YANADI RESPONSE TO CHANGE

YANADI RESPONSE TO CHANGE

An Attempt in Action Anthropology

BINOD C AGRAWAL
N SUDHAKAR RAO
P C GURIVI REDDY

CONCEPT PUBLISHING COMPANY
NEW DELHI

First Published 1985

Published by

Naurang Rai
Concept Publishing Company
H-13, Bali Nagar
NEW DELHI-110015 (India)

Printed by

Mahajan Enterprises
at Sunil Printers
1067, Ajay Palace, Naraina
NEW DELHI 110028

Preface

IN 1970 India decided to put science and technology to work in space in the aid of the country's developmental efforts. The basic infrastructure and other facilities were located about 100 kilometres north of Madras city in the island of Sriharikota. About five years later it all started at a dinner. Professor Satish Dhawan, Chairman, Indian Space Research Organisation (ISRO), was casually asked about the "future plan" of space research in India. He mentioned the activities of Sriharikota (now known as SHAR) and the problems of the tribe Yanadi who, at that time, were returning to SHAR in spite of tight security. The land and the forest of the Yanadi had now become an estate of ISRO. The Yanadi were therefore, no more entitled to live on Sriharikota island or eat the fruits and roots growing on it.

Professor Dhawan asked if anthropological knowledge could help in solving the tribal problem. The reply was "yes" but first SHAR had to be visited. This brief discussion culminated in a remark let fall by Professor Dhawan who said, "Please do something about the Yanadi"

The visit to Yanadi country became a reality. It was a unique experience for the authors to meet a tribe which still produced fire by friction. Driving on the roads of SHAR did not give any clue about the Yanadi and their existence on the island. A few kilometres inside the jungle clusters of inverted betelnut shaped huts made of dried palmyrah leaves called *gudiselu* were found. Here lived the lean Yanadi men in their loin cloths, their women clad only in a piece of cloth wrapped around the torso, their children playing about and chasing insects. All of them seemed to be unaware of and quite unconcerned with the high technology and the new masters that had entered their lives.

It was not the first time that the Chairman, ISRO had shown his deep concern about the Yanadi. The SHAR officials from the beginning were trying to help the Yanadi. Professor E.V. Chitnis, Director, Space Applications Centre, Ahmedabad who first went to select SHAR had observed the initial difficulties of the Engineers and Scientists in adopting the island life along with the Yanadi. Dr. Y.J. Rao, Project Officer, SHAR and his staff had worked out several plans to provide suitable work for the Yanadi. When Agarwal met Dr. Y.J. Rao and his administrative staff during the first visit, they provided various details of their effort in this direction. In doing so, the guiding philosophy of the SHAR officials was that the Yanadi were best in the forest work. Hence all efforts should be made to provide forest related work, like plantation, tree cutting and forest collection. A number of facilities including medical help were extended to the Yanadi on an informal basis by the SHAR officials. Concern for the Yanadi was genuine. But then, it was one of the several important things that was to be done on the island at that juncture of SHAR development.

During the visit it became apparent that the Yanadi and non-Yanadi had no intention of leaving the island in a hurry. SHAR officials pointed out that none of the Yanadi and non-Yanadi believed that they would be forced to leave the island in the near future. For SHAR officials, the future of the Yanadi and non-Yanadi inhabitants was linked with ISRO. The question was how to integrate then into the technical plans and objectives of ISRO. The Yanadi could have been removed from the island through legal means. However there was no doubt that SHAR authorities, out of humanitarian and personal convictions, would not have done it.

Agrawal argued that (i) the large forest wealth of SHAR should be maintained and properly utilised in order to keep the ecological system intact; (ii) the Yanadi and the non-Yanadi should be rehabilitated keeping in mind the technical and scientific objectives; and that (ii) it was essential to conduct action oriented research in order to understand the cultural expectations of the Yanadi and their needs in the light of the needs of ISRO.

A few months later sanction was accorded to the Yanadi Action Research Project limiting its scope to the tribe. The sanction included the appointment of two anthropologists. Of the two experienced anthropologists sanctioned to work on this project, Mr. Bageshwar Singh, Anthropologist, Western Region, Udaipur joined it in June 1976. However, due to linguistic problems it became imperative to select Telugu speaking anthropologists for this project. At this stage it was thought appropriate to select two young anthropologists instead of inviting some senior persons on deputation.

The most crucial element of the project was the selection and training of the two young anthropologists who were expected to carry out the action research. At that time the problem was to find anthropologists willing to live with the Yanadi for a period of two to three years. In response to an initial advertisement a large number of fresh Master's degree holders in anthropology from various universities applied for the job. When called for an interview however, not more than fifty per cent of the fifteen appeared for it. Among these too a few were honest enough to say that they could not remain for such a long period in the field. Others seemed to have no feeling for action anthropology. The two who showed their willingness in action anthropology and who eventually joined us were P.C. Gurivi Reddy and N. Sudhakar Rao who had worked with the poor in rural and urban areas of Andhra Pradesh for about a year. It had given them the much-needed perspective for this unique project. The course of the Yanadi Action Research Project took a new direction after they joined it in November, 1976.

The above details are provided merely as background information to recapitulate the scenario in which the action programme was ushered. What has been described in the following pages is based on our patient and consistent efforts to bring about change in the life of the Yanadi.

Ahmedabad
5 November 1982

BINOD C AGRAWAL

Acknowledgement

THIS BOOK is the outcome of the collective *effort* and *will* of the Yanadi to bring about change in their lives. We like to put on record the gratitude and sincere thanks to all those whose collective effort and wisdom helped the Yanadi to accept the new challenges. First and foremost, we like to thank Professor Satish Dhawan without whose vision this project could not have been conducted.

We are thankful to Col. N. Pant, Mr K.A. Varadan who took personal interest in implementing several of our suggestions and provided encouragement during the entire period of the project. Several other SHAR Centre officials assisted us in many ways. Notable among these were Dr Veeraraju and Mr N. S. Raju. Mr Raghavan and Dr Nagabhushanam took special interest in our efforts to expose the Yanadi to the modern medical system. Far beyond the call of duty, Mr R. B. Singh and the members of the Yanadi Welfare Committee took great pains in implementing several of our suggestions. We would like to thank them for their sustained help. Several state government officials, especially the Block Development Officer, Sulurpetta provided willing assistance whenever the need arose. We are thankful to him and his staff.

The field study was initiated by Mr. Bageshwar Singh, Anthropological Survey of India. He continued his association with this project and participicted at every stage of its implementation. We are sincerely grateful to him for his valuable insight and assistance.

Professors Yash Pal and E. V. Chitnis of this Centre took personal interest in this project. We are sincerely thankful to them for their valuable and timely help. We are also thankful to the staff of the Centre who provided assistance on several occasions, especially Dr Arvind K. Sinha and Mr K. K. Raghavan.

Finally our thanks go to Mr Seshadri for considerable editorial assistance and to Mr Naurang Rai and Mrs S. Ramaswamy of Concept Publishing Company for bringing out this volume.

BINOD C AGRAWAL
N SUDHAKAR RAO
P C GURIVI REDDY

Contents

List of Plates

List of Figures

List of Tables

1

Elements of Action Anthropology

APPLICATIONS of anthropology to solve human problems as also to change human behaviour have been one of the preoccupations of the practitioners. The concepts of 'action' and 'applied' anthropology have been used interchangeably to identify anthropological applications. So far, applications of anthropology have been conceived as a *role* rather than an occupation of anthropologists who in most cases are academics conducting research and acting as advisors, consultants, evaluators, and experts. According to Foster:

> Applied anthropology is the phrase commonly used by anthropologists to describe their professional activities in programmes that have as primary goals changes in human behaviour believed to ameliorate contemporary social, economic and technological problems rather than development of social and cultural theory.[1]

There seems to be some difference of opinion about the role of applications of anthropology. Mair (1968) views it as an extension of the on-going research activities for the purposes of decision-making, whereas anthropologists like Clifton (1970), Tax (1970), and Bastide (1973), consider it is an action-oriented application of anthropology. In short, they perceive applications of anthropology as 'learning through action' (Peddington 1970:135). They see this action orientation as not divorced from pure research. Peddington summarizes the whole orientation thus :

> As a scientific discipline, action anthropology is clinical

> rather than predictive. It does not aim to apply general anthropological principles directly to a body of observational data existing at any one time so as to produce a 'blue print' for the future... Instead, by picking up a series of cues (in the light of general principles, of course) it allows concrete plans for action to emerge progressively from the on-going process of social change.[2]

Indian studies on action anthropology are very scanty. Naik (1972) and Vidyarthi (1978) reported that majority of the researches classified as 'applied anthropology' envisaged the anthropologist's role as 'consultant', 'advisor', 'co-ordinator' and 'evaluator'. Naik's review of nearly 175 studies shows that most of the studies are either 'evaluative' or 'suggestive'. His study also indicates that there has been no attempt to define action anthropology or to describe the role of anthropologists or to delineate the methodology for action programmes in the Indian context.

In the contemporary professional arena, action anthropology has been enjoying the dubious distinction of being labelled *research* sometimes second rate on the one hand, and sometimes unethical *intervention* in the life of others on the other hand. The former activity stems from a 'value free' notion of anthropology, which the authors argue does not exist. We believe that anthropologists who study humans can better help in bringing about desirable change than those whose research gives them the deep understanding of human cultures, problems and needs. Thus, one can take two interrelated but distinct approaches for the applications of anthropology. In the first role, the anthropologist can gather 'facts', diagnose the problems, and suggest possible solutions which are to be implemented by somebody else. Here the anthropologist assumes the role of an advisor, consultant, evaluator, and expert. In the second role, the anthropologist, after gathering facts, diagnoses the problem, suggests alternative strategies, and helps in actualizing the suggested solutions by choosing one of the most appropriate alternatives. Even before suggesting any solution, the anthropologist, confers, discusses, and mobilizes opinion as to what should be the viable alternatives to bring about desirable changes. The desirability is defined in terms of what the people think is essential for their betterment. While changes are induced, the anthropologist tries to evaluate whether the desirable changes are taking place and if necessary, suggests modifications or implements alternative solutions.

We have followed the second approach and used the label 'action anthropology' to describe our experiences. When we started working on the Yanadi Action Research Project, we strongly felt that by simply suggesting solutions to the problems and remaining as consultants and advisors desirable changes would not be brought about among the Yanadi. Hence, continued association of the anthropologist was considered desirable till our goal was achieved.

Action research paradigm

Initially our role in the project was limited to suggesting solutions. This involved a study of the Yanadi culture and their problems and their needs. However, very soon it was realized that a passive role would not help the Yanadi in alleviating their misery, poverty, and frustration. This led to the broadening of the scope of the project and redefining our role as (a) implementers of ideas, (b) consciousness-raisers of the Yanadi, and (c) link between the Yanadi and the SHAR administration and other developmental agencies.

After broadening the scope of our activity, we started looking for some paradigm for action. Since we could not find one, we evolved our own (see Fig. 1). Its philosophy is that introduction of any change must lead to increased self-reliance and not to loss of identity. It assumes a dual role for the anthropologist : researcher and change agent. The role of the researcher is close to what most anthropologists do i.e. to study the culture and to evaluate the needs and problems. However, two subsequent steps are quite close to the applied anthropologist's role i.e. prioritization of needs and problems, and suggesting solutions. Up to this point, anthropologists in most parts of the world would accept our action paradigm.

Anthropologists are confronted with a very different kind of problem in the role of a change agent. They are expected to examine suggested solutions. This step is quite crucial, as it involves evaluation of client agencies and financial resources and their ideological stances. At the same time, it involves developing a strategy for introducing change, which requires a careful analysis of the situation, readiness of the community to accept new ideas, and ability to motivate or influence the

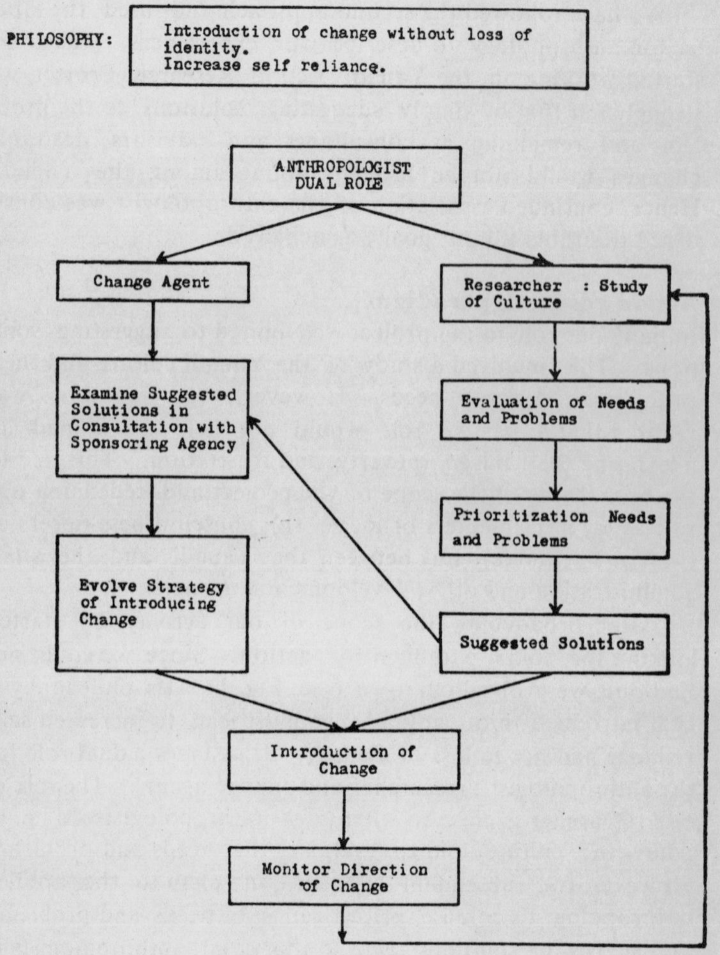

FIG. 1 : *Action Paradigm*

community to accept them. Continuous monitoring, evaluation, and re-study of the culture are important components of any action programme.

Again in the researcher's role, the anthropologist evaluates the effects of induced change. The results of the study are expected to help the change agent in modifying, redesigning, and terminating undesirable elements of change as far as possible. Although it is essential to separate the two roles for conceptual clarity yet, in reality, the authors found that the two roles were complementary and inseparable.

Problems of change agent role

As change agents, we were confronted with a very different kind of situation. The suggestions of earlier anthropologists were re-examined in the light of new data. Some of the action programmes were rejected and a few others were modified.

Apart from being professional anthropologists, we also belonged to a large scientific organisation, with number of rules and regulations necessary for running the system. In this system, there are laid out procedures for implementing decisions. For example, the purchase of any item requires 8 to 12 weeks. We were expected to follow the existing procedure as this action project was to be implemented through SHAR administration. In the process, we found it difficult at times, to directly approach decision makers for quick action.

Our eagerness to help the Yanadi at times, led others to consider us brethrens of Yanadi, rather than as protectors of the interests of ISRO. At times it appeared to us as if all our ideals were shattered. As pragmatists, on such occasions, we negotiated, compromised, and yielded in order to safeguard Yanadi interests. But we did all this with a clear conscience; we believed that it would help the Yanadi in the long run.

We had a number of advantages also in the implementation of our action plans since we were part of the same organization. Due to the keen interest taken by the Chairman of ISRO and the Director and Controller of SHAR, we often had easier access to them and we were able to get our ideas carried out through them. As Agrawal lived away from SHAR, this access had helped in providing freedom to Gurivi Reddy and Sudhakar Rao in making independent decisions, but it had also generated a certain sense of insecurity among them.

Anthropologists in the field

A very short and preliminary field work among the Yanadi was conducted in the latter half of 1975 by Agrawal when he visited eight Yanadi habitations during the course of his stay. He observed the Yanadi way of life, interaction with the non-Yanadi, and their periodic movements on the island. He interviewed them with the help of an interpreter and suggested short-term solutions.

Bageshwar Singh's field work began in June 1976 after the project was sanctioned. He observed the Yanadi behaviour and conducted indepth interviews with the help of interpreters. He also discussed the project with several anthropologists to steer it in the right direction. Because of language difficulty, he could not directly communicate with the Yanadi. At the same time Agrawal visited the island and there was a high level meeting about the project. In the meeting, Agrawal and Singh suggested some action programmes. Singh could get some of the action programmes implemented in late 1976. Active field work began at the end of 1976 when the two Telugu-speaking anthropologists entered the scene. The two anthropologists were surprised to find small, low and round huts in clusters in the midst of thick forests. Their assumption was that the Yanadi island would resemble the mainland Yanadi. But they were bewildered to meet tall, lean and dark Yanadi with minimum clothing and uncared for curly hair. To a large extent the rapport established by the earlier anthropologists helped Gurivi Reddy and Sudhakar Rao to introduce themselves to the Yanadi.

To get acquainted with the Yanadi, the anthropologists started taking a census. They could contact them in the evening after they returned from work. The response, however, was poor as the Yanadi felt exhausted after a day's hard labour. Therefore, the Yanadi's holidays were fruitfully used to collect the census and genealogical data. Several months of continuous interaction with the Yanadi led the anthropologists to the realization that in the beginning the Yanadi had concealed some relevant information especially regarding their re-marriages and divorces.

In order to have an understanding of different groups of the Yanadi, it was felt that one of the two anthropologists should live in a place inhabited exclusively by the Yanadi whereas the other should live in a mixed habitation of both Yanadi and non-Yanadi. It was further felt that, it would help to cross check their data. Accordingly, the two anthropologists began to live, from February 1977, in two of the eight habitations. However, they visited other habitations frequently.

The Yanadi very often talked to the anthropologists voluntarily. That was only when they had any personal problem, which is quite characteristic of their behaviour. Otherwise, they rarely visited the anthropologists. So the anthropologists generally visited Yanadi huts even for informal talks. It was observed that the Yanadi could not give sufficient information on any particular aspect of their culture in an interview situation. However, such information could easily be gathered while participating in their day-to-day life. Thus, the anthropologists used methods of participant observation and interviews. While participating in the day-to-day activities informal interviews were found to be very helpful. Women were less communicative than men. However, a few elderly women were relatively free to talk. Through them, important data concerning women were collected. The grown-up boys were frequent visitors to anthropologists and they were good sources for some useful data.

Typically, the day for the anthropologists began when the women got up to cook. On winter mornings, men, children and occasionally women gathered around camp fires. Participation in these gatherings allowed the anthropologists to hear the exchange of Yanadi experiences about hunting, fishing, gathering and encounters with the non-Yanadi and their jokes. The anthropologists accompanied the Yanadi to their work. This helped to understand the Yanadi work behaviour, their relationships with 'employers' and work and possible methods of exploitation by the 'employers'. On these occasions, the employers of the Yanadi were also interviewed to collect their impressions about the Yanadi.

In the habitations, the anthropologists spent most of the

time with the children and grown-up boys and girls. They observed extensively the Yanadi pattern of forest food collection, interaction and participation in the games, hunting and fishing. Most of the evenings were spent with adult men and women in informal talks and group discussions. While talking to them in their huts, the anthropologists observed their way of cooking, and using food ingredients and method of food distribution among household members. After their evening meals, the children of the nearby huts gathered in a separate hut to sleep. There they sang songs and exchanged riddles till they fell asleep. They also performed *malam* (see Chapter 4). The boys would also narrate their sexual experiences, information about divorces, re-marriages, and actual reasons for quarrels which were generally not talked about openly. The anthropologists observed *rangam* (see Chapter 6) on a number of occasions. The performance was meant to cure diseases by invoking their gods. Probing deep into the *rangam* performance helped to understand the entire Yanadi belief system and how their way of life centred around it. This contributed much to understand the Yanadi world. The continuous and close interaction and participation in most of their activities gave a deep understanding of the culture, the problems they faced and the needs to be fulfilled.

REFERENCES

1. George M. Foster, *Applied Anthropology*, p. 64.
2. Ralph Peddington, Action Anthropology *in* James A Cliffton (ed.) *Applied Anthropology*, pp.135-36.

2

Yanadi in Historical Perspective

UNTIL 1970, Sriharikota could be approached by country boats from the small coastal town of Tada, situated on the Nellore-Madras Grand Trunk Road. Usually, open boats carried passengers from Tada to Venadu, Irakam and Sriharikota islands. The journey to Sriharikota was generally made around midnight to take advantage of the wind and the high water line. The crew waited at Tada for the onset of the land breeze. The island could be reached in three hours, if the wind was favourable, otherwise it took ten to twelve hours to cover a distance of twenty nine kilometres. The Buckingham Canal passes along the western edge of the Sriharikota island and is separated by a bund from the Pulicat Lake. There is no direct access to the Buckingham Canal from the lake. Hence the passengers used to change to other boats plying in the canal. The journey in the canal was uneventful and even monotonous because of the bad odour from stagnant waters. The scenery of the island is varied and picturesque with abundant vegetation and extensive jungles honeycombed with plantations of eucalyptus and casuarina, numerous groves of coconut palms and cane brooks around ponds.

The return journey commenced around 12 noon when the sea breeze started to blow. It was not at any rate as interesting as the onward journey by night. Tada was reached by the same route around 5 p.m. if the wind was favourable and around 7 p.m. if it was unfavourable. During summer, Sriharikota could be reached from the northern side as the lake dried.

Transportation in the Island

The transportation system established by the British for

carrying forest produce, consisted of the trolleys pushed by men on the rails. Important places of the island were connected by this rail system. Till 1970, this facility was used by the forest department for their own transportation. However, the non-Yanadi used bullock carts to cover small distances. Firewood was carried on boats to Madras through the Buckingham Canal. However, the construction of a road connecting the island with the mainland in 1970, was a major event in the history of the island and its population. For the first time, Sriharikota became a part of large landmass and lost its relative isolation and the distinction of being an 'island' in the Bay of Bengal. It was the beginning of a new chapter in the lives of inhabitants of Sriharikota.

Topography and soils

The soils of Sriharikota are sandy and are marine and aeolian in nature, rising more than 4.5 to 6.0 metres above sea level. Under thick vegetation, there are soils with good admixture of humus and sand. The coast stretches to half a kilometre from the shore and another half a kilometre stretch of bare sand which is uneven and consists of *dibbalu* (mounds) rising to 3.0 to 4.5 metres. They are the result of wind erosion. On the northern and southern parts of the island, there are sand dunes which range in height from 4.5 to 6.0 metres above sea level.

Peddavagu and Chinnavagu are streams which run parallel to the seashore. Water in these streams is sweet. Near the sea coast, the water table is about 3.5 metres and in other parts it is about 2.0 metres. According to Yanadi belief, stream water is considered fit for drinking. Apart from these are *daruvulu* (fresh water sources) along the western edge of the island. *Daruvulu* had been used for paddy cultivation in the past (Rao 1970).

Climate

The year round 'warm' climate is tempered by the moderating influence of the sea breeze from the Bay of Bengal and the Pulicat Lake. The climate can be said to be equable. The sands of the island become refractory during summer, making the climate humid and oppressive (Rao 1970). The maximmu temperature is recorded in May and the minimum in February. The maximum temperature recorded is as high as (43.5°C) and as low as 13.5°C during the period 1975-77. Variation in the mean minimum and maximum temperatures is low. Rains are recorded in October and November. During the south-west monsoon season, the island gets moderate rainfall. The average annual rainfall in the period 1975-77 was 1355.6 mm. The island is prone to cyclones, especially in the early part of May when the south-west monsoon sets in and again with the onset of north-east monsoon in October (SHAR 1979).

Flora and fauna

The major portion of the island is covered with dense evergreen scrub forests. However, in certain regions, thick vegetation is found due to admixture of humus with sand. The indigenous growth was replaced by the introduction of exotic species such as casuarina, eucalyptus and cashew tree plantations in the mid-nineteenth century. The forest is rich in different kinds of herbs and tubers which the Yanadi use as medicines. Based on a study during 1976-77, the famous ornithologist, Salim Ali estimated the existence of about 115 species of birds. Among them, there are different migrating birds. *Varanus*, wild boar, Indian jackal, black naped hare, mongoose, bonnet macaque, three striped squirrel and other species of wild life are also found on the island.

Yanadi in British period

The earliest reference to the Yanadi is found in 1835, when *mutta* (area) of Sriharikota came into the possession of the British government (Nellore Manual : Letter No. 22.9). The British officials described the Yanadi as "wild" and a "peculiar" tribe or race. The British employed the Yanadi as labourers to collect the jungle produce and also cut firewood. The British officials have also recorded the living conditions of this tribe. But the information they collected had been through local authorities such as tahsildars and collectors leaving a lot to be desired about the quality of data. An analysis based on the 'impressionistic' and 'biased' information about the Yanadi as described by the British officials is presented with a view that it would throw some light on the socio-economic conditions of the Yanadi in the mid-nineteenth century.

The Yanadi were rarely seen by outsiders as they dwelled in the interiors of the forest and were in a state of "barbarism' (Nellore Manual : Letter No. 22.9). They were dependent on fruits, roots and other jungle products. The Yanadi of Sriharikota were referred to as *government Yanadi* by the British officials distinguishing them from the mainland (Nellore Manual : Letter No. 21). To restrict the wandering habits of the Yanadi the British introduced a legislation by which all marriages were registered and premiums on births were given (Nellore Manual: Letter No. 22). The British also introduced clothes, rice and tobacco to the Yanadi (Nellore Manual : Letter No. 1).

The Yanadi were filthy in the extreme. The men had nothing on but a *longoti* (loin cloth) and the women wore the barest rag of a cloth. The men tied their hair up in a knot usually on the top of the head whereas the women let their hair loose. Their huts were mere circular frames of sticks usually two metres in diameter and thatched with palmyrah leaves. They used to crawl into the huts like pigs. But for a few pots and fowl their material possessions were meagre. Their idea of religion was the crudest and most primitive in nature. The God in vogue was called *Chenchu Devudu* (the wild or savage God) a name obviously given by others than his own votaries (Nellore Manual : Letter No. 22). Marriages were based on consent of the man and woman. The relatives and friends were not consulted in fixing a marriage. This was possible because the Yanadi women did marry before attaining puberty. After the wedding betel leaves and nuts were distributed; the marriage string was tied around the bride's neck; and the bride was taken to the husband's house.

The British government felt the need to educate the Yanadi children towards the eventual civilization and consequent welfare of the tribe. It was hoped that the children would be found willing to attend the school. Thus those Yanadi might gradually be weaned from their present habitat and brought into an intercourse with their more civilized neighbours. A school was opened in 1858 with one teacher but it was closed down in 1877 owing to poor attendance. The government felt that the Yanadi might be trained in useful occupations such as fishing, agriculture and forest employment and stationary pursuits. But all the attempts failed because the Yanadi did not take any interest (Nellore Manual : Letter No. 21 and 22; Thurston 1909 : 418). Thurston also makes a similar observation :

> The animistic nature of their religion, the production of fire by friction, the primitive hunting and fishing stage in which a large number remain, the almost raw animal food which they eat, after merely scorching or heating the flesh of the game they kill, indicate that the Yanadi have not emerged from a primitive stage of culture.[1]

We have no information about the effect of British efforts in changing the Yanadi way of life. However, the measures did somewhat increase the Yanadi interaction with the non-Yanadi of the island. It was observed that older Yanadi had more interaction with their neighbours. The necessity of bringing forest produce to the *kacheri* (office) necessarily brought them face to face with non-Yanadi neighbours. A certain amount of interaction with others was possible since payment was made in cash.

Yanadi population in Sriharikota

The Yanadi are the second largest tribe in Andhra Pradesh

TABLE 2.1 : VILLAGE-WISE DISTRIBUTION OF YANADI POPULATION

Village	1961			1971		
	Male	Female	Total	Male	Female	Total
Chantrasikuppam	21	21	42	24	20	44
Kondaledu	86	57	143	90	63	153
Chengalpalem	11	11	22	45	95	140
Doravaripalem	188	133	321	80	58	138
Kalavagu	25	19	44	—	—	—
Beripeta	178	159	337	178	158	336
Rettamala	35	39	74	27	23	50
Chennugaripalem	34	30	64	6	3	9
Total	578	469	1,047	450	420	870

SOURCE : *Census of India*, 1961 and 1971.

with a population of 2,39,409 (*Census of India*, 1971). Nearly fifty per cent of them live in Nellore district alone. The Yanadi of Sriharikota constituted about one per cent of the total district population as per 1971 Census. Village-wise distribution of the Yanadi population in Sriharikota in 1961 and 1971 is given in Table 2.1.

One can easily see the preponderance of male population over females. Another interesting feature is the decreasing Yanadi population which may be attributed to the total population's evacuation from the island. In 1977, when a fresh census was taken, only 519 Yanadi remained on the island. There is no information as to where the remaining Yanadi went between 1971 and 1977. It is presumed that they migrated to new villages or got lost in the maze of mainland living or perished after leaving the island.

TABLE 2.2 : CAMP-WISE POPULATION IN 1977

Name of the Camp	Number of Households			Male	Female	Total
	Sarkar	Raithu	Total			
Keepakam	13	8	21	42	35	77
Penubakam	—	16	16	30	25	55
Maulam	13	13	26	57	41	98
BN Road	—	8	8	21	17	38
Solladaruvu	19	6	25	47	44	91
Kalavagu	1	15	16	36	32	68
Pitcharigunta	4	11	15	39	29	68
Kernalapalem	—	7	7	14	10	24
Total	50	84	134	286	233	519

SOURCE : Actual enumeration conducted by the authors.

The Yanadi lived in eight labour camps in small clusters of huts of around two dozen households at any one locale. SHAR authorities called these Yanadi settlements "labour camps" signifying the temporary nature of their habitation. These temporary labour camps moved in various parts of the island depending upon the forest work requirements. The Yanadi especially those working in the forestry and horticulture section of SHAR led a nomadic life in the island. In a way this life was not dissimilar to their past life pattern.

Prior to 1970, the Yanadi lived with other Hindu *jatis* like Reddy, Berisetty, Eendra, Golla, Pattapu, Chakali, Mangali and Mala. A few Muslims were also observed living in two of these villages. Among all, the Reddy *jati* cultivators were numerically and economically the most dominant. A somewhat similar settlement pattern continued even in 1975. The Yanadi identified themselves as *Sarkar* (government) or *Raithu* (cultivator) Yanadi. Numerically there were more Raithu Yanadi (little over 60 per cent) than Sarkar Yanadi households (little less than 40 per cent) (Table 2.2). Though there had been few marriages between them, the Sarkar and Raithu Yanadi maintained physical as well as social distance and had little interaction in the past owing to the Raithu Yanadi feeling superior to the Sarkar Yanadi.

Sarkar Yanadi

The interaction of Sarkar Yanadi with non-Yanadi was mostly through the state forest department officials. The officials were accorded the status of 'teachers'. They taught the Yanadi to wash clothes, clean themselves, cook the food properly, and conduct various rituals. The Yanadi were also introduced to Muslim saints by the forest officials. The relationship between the forest officials and the Yanadi was very cordial. The officials were lending money and settling their disputes often. The State Forest Department was running a cooperative provision store where the Yanadi could buy food items. Once in six months, each adult was given a pair of *dhotis* (wrap-around garment for men) or *saris* (length of material to drape around for women) by the State Forest Department.

The Forest Ranger used to appoint a headman (*maestri*) whose duty it was to make the Yanadi work regularly, settle all their disputes and maintain harmony. To assist the *maestri* three deputy headmen (*thinethulu*) were appointed who lived at Beripeta, Ponna and Maulam, and were in charge of the Yanadi living in their localities. They were to supervise the rest of the Yanadi at workspots and report to the forester for day-to-day duties. The *maestri* and *thinethulu* had been severely beating the Yanadi for minor mistakes and offences such as absenting from work, joining the Reddys for work, extra-marital relations and for not giving proper respect and obeying orders. Several Yanadi unable to withstand the harsh treatment had committed suicide by consuming a poisonous tuber. Often the *maestri*, after getting drunk would forcibly have sexual relations with the Sarkar Yanadi women of his choice. No Sarkar Yanadi was bold enough to complain against their headman.

The Sarkar Yanadi were engaged in works such as planting, digging ditches, transplantation, and collecting seasonal forest produce such as *musti* fruits, tamarind, soapnut and *sugandha pala* on daily wage basis. They worked from early morning to evening. However, they were permitted during noon to go to interiors of the forest and collect tubers and fruits and catch small game. At the time of evacuation, the daily wages paid to an adult man, a woman and child were Rs. 3.0, Rs. 2.50 and Rs. 1.50 respectively. Payments were made according to the amount of collection. Generally, wages were transferred directly to the co-operative stores where the Sarkar Yanadi could buy the rations. A sum of four to five rupees a weak was paid to them in cash.

A few of the Sarkar Yanadi worked as watchmen and guards and were paid monthly. These Sarkar Yanadi had to visit the non-Yanadi villages in connection with their duties. The rich Reddys of these villages maintained very cordial relations with these Sarkar Yanadi by offering liquor and toddy freely in return for permitting such illicit activities as timber smuggling and stealing forest produce.

There was a school at Kothachenu with free boarding and lodging facilities but very few Sarkar Yanadi attended it. Similarly the hospital at Beripeta was never visited by them. No Yanadi was ever vaccinated. Thus, we observe a relative isolation, dependence on the forest officials and minimum interaction with the non-Yanadi among the Sarkar Yanadi.

Raithu Yanadi

The life of the Raithu Yanadi was somewhat better than that of the Sarkar Yanadi. In each village, the Raithu Yanadi lived in the neighbourhood of the non-Yanadi. Generally, many households belonging to an *intiperu* (household name) and a few households of another *intiperu* lived together. Marriages had been taking place mainly between the two *intiperu* of these households. Each of these *intiperu* had a headman (*maestri*) to maintain harmonious living and to resolve disputes. These Yanadi had been frequently leaving the village and going to different places, generally inside the island, and rarely outside the island to work for the non-Yanadi. A few households at Jonangipalem earned their living from fishing in the Pulicat Lake and the Buckingham Canal. In some villages, some women worked as maid servants and male children tended the cattle of the Reddys. Very few Yanadi ever worked as full time servants or as bonded labour.

Every year, the Forest Department used to auction some coups of casuarina and eucalyptus. The rich Reddys and other non-Yanadi of the island and outsiders engaged the Raithu Yanadi for felling the coups and exporting the pieces to Madras. The felling and cutting used to take place throughout the year. After a piece of work generally the rich contractors used to give a feast of goat's meat and liquor to the Yanadi. Some of them gave them *dhotis* and *saris* also. Some of the regular contractors used to have a group of Raithu Yanadi to work for them for long periods whenever they got the contract.

Women and children also helped the men in cutting operations. There were no fixed hours of work; whenever the Raithu Yanadi felt like working they did so. They were paid Rs. 10 to 15 for cutting one tonne of wood which was measured in quantity and not by weight. Generally, the contractors, instead of paying cash, provided them with rice and other provisions in advance. The contractor used to look after the welfare of the Raithu Yanadi and provide food in the case of sickness. In most cases, the Raithu Yanadi could not clear the advances. But then advances were given in such a way that a Raithu Yanadi could never be able to repay them. In this disguised patronage the Raithu Yanadi were heavily exploited by extracting from them high quantum of wood, selling rice at higher rates, and making wrong calculations on their wages which the Yanadi could never do by themselves.

The Raithu Yanadi were engaged by the non-Yanadi for

Hindu rituals and other odd jobs where they learned about Hindu ceremonies and rituals. There had been sexual liaison between the Yanadi and the non-Yanadi. The non-Yanadi in a few cases kept Yanadi women as concubines and in a few cases married them. Some Raithu Yanadi men also had sex relations with non-Yanadi women. When the Raithu Yanadi were unable to settle their disputes they approached the non-Yanadi elders of the village council. The Raithu Yanadi were also invited as 'members' to the village Panchayat, though there were no formal elections. Although relations of the Raithu Yanadi with the non-Yanadi were congenial, the Raithu Yanadi were placed in an inferior social position compared to the Reddys and many other *jatis*. The Yanadi were expected to remove their wooden sandals in front of a Reddy and were expected to keep some distance while walking with a Reddy. A Raithu Yanadi had to stand still when a Reddy passed by, further the Reddy had to be given way. The Raithu Yanadi were not expected to smoke a beedi or spit in front of a Reddy. The Yanadi were severely beaten by the Reddys if they violated these 'codes of behaviour'.

Very few of the Raithu Yanadi children went to the school. They could study only up to fifth grade as they could not leave the island for further studies. After the evacuation of the inhabitants of the island, the school at Jonangipalem was shifted to a village near Gudur, nearly 60 kilometres from Sriharikota. The headmaster of the school took two Yanadi boys along with him to the new village. One of the two boys could study up to the tenth grade whereas the other discontinued his studies in the seventh grade and returned to the island. In the school, the Raithu Yanadi children had very close interaction with the non-Yanadi children and teachers. In the school, they learnt cleanliness, apart from reading and writing of Telugu. Even these educated Yanadi seldom visited the hospital at Beripeta.

Comparison between Sarkar and Raithu Yanadi

Relatively speaking, interaction between the Raithu Yanadi and the non-Yanadi was higher compared to the Sarkar Yanadi. The Raithu Yanadi worked with other non-Yanadi labourers of the contractors which resulted in close contacts and relations. They were frequent visitors of liquor, provision and other shops and used to participate in the rituals, ceremonies and festivals of the non-Yanadi. Comparatively, the Raithu Yanadi were earning more than the Sarkar Yanadi, but they were spending mostly on country liquor and toddy sold by the non-Yanadi. The Sarkar and Raithu Yanadi needed cooperation of their kin-group during religious ceremonies.

The Yanadi used mostly earthen pots which were sold at Kasapai village outside the island. Fire was produced by friction. Apart from rice, all Yanadi enjoyed eating a variety of forest produce which included nearly seventeen kinds of wild fruits, ten kinds of tubers, four types of seeds and eight varieties of leaves which were directly consumed but not sold to others. Among these, *yellagaddalu* (stamen tubers) and palmyrah (*Borassus flabelliformis*) were consumed in very large quantities. The evening meals of both Yanadi quite often consisted of rice and fish, meat of the hunt and, occasionally, cooked leaves of the forest. Honey was given to infants. It was also used for treating burns.

The Yanadi could identify the footprints of their relatives, neighbours and animals and birds. Animals were caught by identifying their footprints disturbing the shelter and chasing them with the help of dogs. When sick, the Yanadi conducted *rangam* to invoke their gods to cure their ailments. In addition, they also used some medicinal herbs. Sankranti and Deepavali were the two festivals celebrated by these Yanadi.

Yanadi after evacuation

The term Yanadi now onwards refers to both Sarkar and Raithu Yanadi unless specified. After the takeover of the island, ISRO started constructing laboratories, workshops, offices, roads and other establishments. Those Yanadi who had initially resisted the pressure to leave could easily get employment with ISRO for clearing the jungle, cutting cane groves and collecting forest produce. Most of these works were given against tendered contracts. The contractors hired these Yanadi and when they needed more labourers they brought Yanadi from rehabilitated villages who were familiar with the work and the island's geography.

The new 'villages' where the Yanadi were rehabilitated in 1970 were poorly managed. There was an acute shortage of water. The Yanadi were given land for cultivation but they did not know cultivation. The compensation of Rs. 500 given at the time of evacuation was over within a week in the new place (mostly because of cheating by liquor sellers). Several Yanadi suffered from diseases and died. Many starved for several days. The net result was that many Yanadi returned to the island. Those Yanadi who came to work for the contractors also stayed back, even though they were without work.

The SHAR officials were concerned at the reappearance of the Yanadi on the island. Almost five years passed by in the process without any serious efforts to tackle the Yanadi problem. In these five years, the Yanadi faced numerous, new unanticipated hardships and difficulties. These included the encounters with many unknown ISRO officials, new contractors and above all the security guards, who were very different from those of the old forest guards. From now on our focus will be on the 519 Yanadi who continued to live on the island.

REFERENCE

1. E. Thurston. *Castes and Tribes of South India.* Vol. VII, p. 417.

Yanadi in Socio-Cultural Perspective

FURTHER ANALYSIS of Yanadi culture is presented in this chapter using the 'world view' approach. The term world view encompasses the forms of thought, comprehensive attitude towards life, structural arrangement of beings and principles (Redfield 1953, 1955). It is hoped that such an analysis would help understand the needs and problems of the Yanadi in changed circumstances.

Yanadi world view

The Yanadi forms of thought and structural arrangements are dichotomous in nature. This dichotomy makes itself manifest in the Yanadi attitude towards life and various relationships with men, animals, plants, gods and devils. The Yanadi consider that the earth is very huge in a semi-circular bridge shape. They believe that the west and south of the

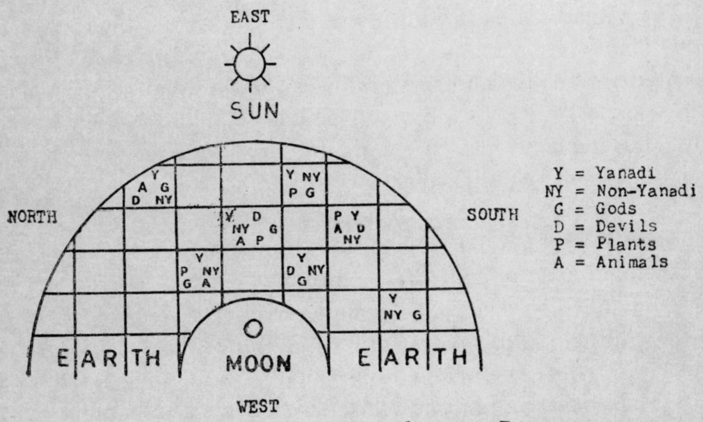

FIG. 2 : *Yanadi Habitation Pattern*

earth are more elevated than the east and north. The sun and moon revolve around the static earth.

According to the Yanadi, the world is divided into *naralokam* (visible world of human beings) and *dibalokam* (invisible world on the earth). The only difference between the two is that in the *naralokam* human beings can be seen with naked eyes whereas in *dibalokam* they are invisible. When one of these two worlds is active, the other remains at rest. When it is day in *naralokam*, it is night for the inhabitants of *dibalokam* and vice-versa.

Each block in Figure 2 conceptually separates various habitants on the earth. In each habitation, the gods live either to the south or in the west of direction of the Yanadi, whereas the devils live in the north or eastern the gods. The gods and the non-Yanadi who are superior to the Yanadi live in elevated locales (*eguva*) which are to the west or south of the Yanadi habitation. The habitation pattern indicates the inferiority of the Yanadi to the gods and the non-Yanadi.

Figure 3 categorises the benign and malign living beings in the *naralokam* and *dibalokam*. The benign beings are represented by a positive sign and the malign with the negative sign. The *dibalokam* constitutes the gods and devils. The Yanadi's gods include some of the gods of the Hindu pantheon as well as the dead. Lord Brahma is the highest among the gods, Venkateswara and Chenchamma have equal status and are the most powerful. Among devils, the Dhurthulu is the most powerful followed by Shakthulu.

The Yanadi co-exist with plants and animals in the *naralokkam*. Plants are mainly of two types: salubrious, helpful in maintaining health and curing illness; and insalubrious, which bring sickness, disease and death. Similarly animals are divided into those which can be eaten and are harmless and those which are harmful and dangerous to approach.

The Yanadi consider themselves as 'poor', 'innocent', and 'ignorant' of many matters of the non-Yanadi, whereas the non-Yanadi are thought of as 'prudent', 'aggressive', 'rich', and 'intelligent'. The non-Yanadi are further divided into those who help and protect the Yanadi and those who cheat and harm them. The benign non-Yanadi are identified as closer to gods and the malign ones closer to devils. The benign non-Yanadi maintain the patron-client relationship with the Yanadi

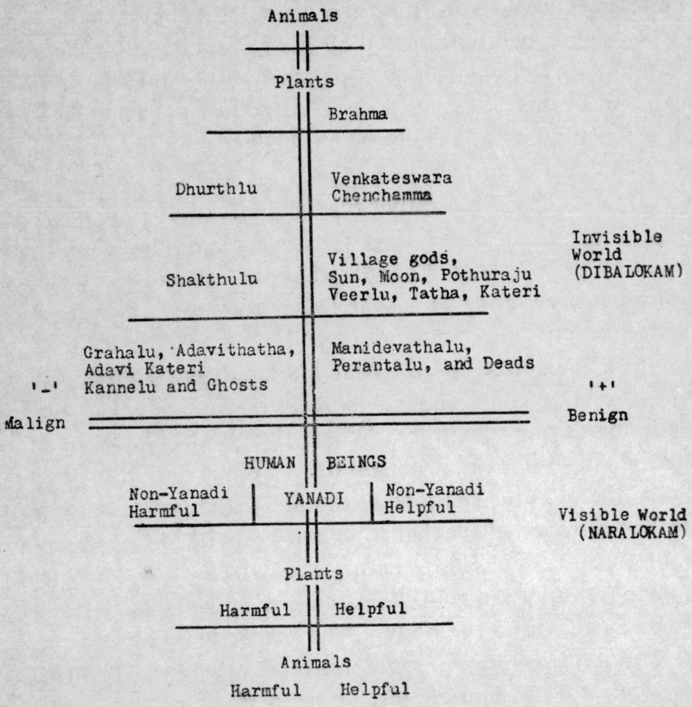

FIG. 3 : *Yanadi Categorization of Beings*

by extending help to them. At the same time they chide, scold, and censure in order to control the Yanadi. The malign non-Yanadi do not have such patron-client relationships.

The Yanadi consider that the benign non-Yanadi are superior to the malign non-Yanadi. So, whenever the malign non-Yanadi harass, the Yanadi approach the benign non-Yanadi for help because the benign non-Yanadi can squarely face the malign non-Yanadi and free the Yanadi from the clutches of the malign non-Yanadi. When the benign non-Yanadi cannot help them, the Yanadi submit themselves to the malign non-Yanadi. Hence, the Yanadi try to maintain close contacts with the benign non-Yanadi and avoid the malign non-Yanadi.

Every Yanadi is named after a god or goddess within a few days after birth. The god consents to take care of the child until death. The god helps the Yanadi to have happy living by providing plants and animals and saving them from all imminent dangers. Thus, the Yanadi believe that every one of them is being protected by the personal god. The personal god not only helps but also punishes by inflicting diseases on the individual if a mistake is committed. The personal god gets annoyed especially when his/her child is beaten by cane, sandals, or broom, kicked by foot and forced to do any menial job. The child rather than the offender is punished by the personal god. Just like gods, the benign non-Yanadi help as well as penalise the Yanadi when the Yanadi misbehave. Punishment by gods is in the form of diseases but the non-Yanadi therely chide and censure.

When a person sleeps, the head life (*yathabondi*) of the person leaves the body and wanders wherever the individual had been wandering during daytime. When the ghosts (*deyyam*) catch hold and devour it, that person dies. When the ghosts catch hold of the invisible shadow of the body, the person falls sick. The Yanadi also believe that a person gets sick owing to biological imbalances caused by eating wrong food. For the Yanadi, to diagnose other kinds of illness caused by gods and/or devils or developed within the body. The *ranakadu* (diviner) is requested to perform *rangam*. On an average there is a diviner for every four to five households. For performing *rangam*, the diviner and his wife first take a bath and then enter their temple hut. Inside the hut, the woman lights a small fire near the entrance. The diviner sits in the centre of the hut in front of the fire, keeping a knee up and drawing the foot close to him whereas the other leg is kept flat on the ground folding towards him. He closes his eyes and sings in praise of gods and his ancestors. The woman sits near the entrance of the hut and keeps on kindling the fire, often adding frankinsence to fire. She keeps on repeating whatever the diviner sings. The diviner continuously sings with breaks for repetition. After some time, he becomes semi-conscious but he keeps on singing and start talking to gods and dead elders who are supposedly seen by him alone. When all the gods appear and are gathered near him he asks them why so and so has fallen sick.

The gods would reveals him the reason for the illness. Revelations are made by indicating the cause of illness such as breach of norms of gods or an act of *deyyalu* (devils) or due to disagreeable food. Accordingly, the ailing person is told to perform a ritual and appease the gods if it is due to indignation of the gods. In the case of absence of *yathabondi* or shadow, the diviner conducts another performance wherein gods are requested to search the *deyyalu*, raid over devils and bring

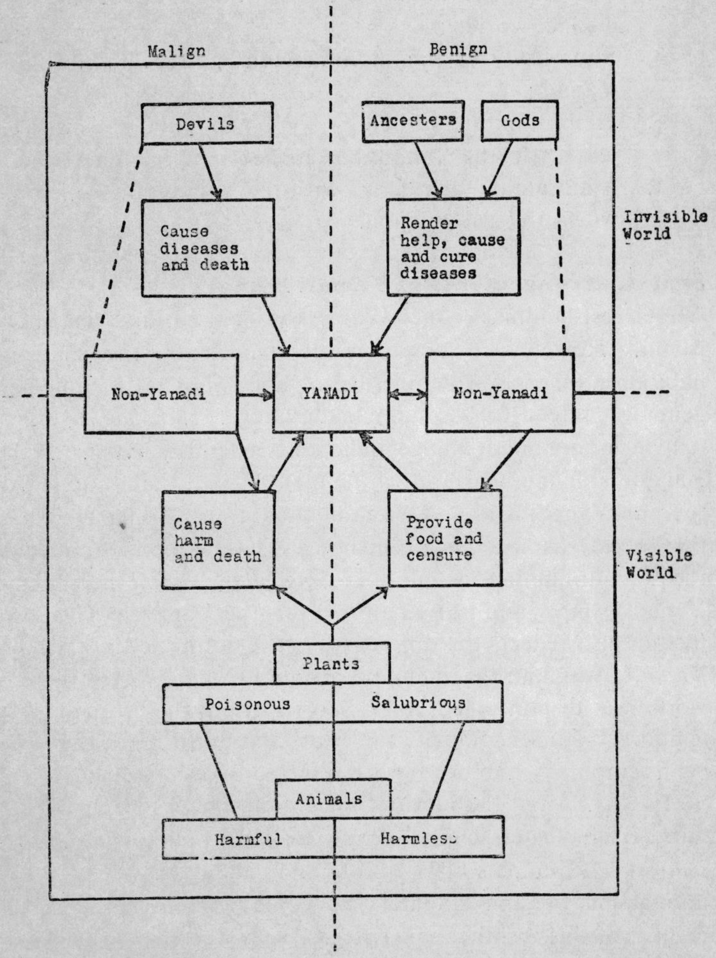

FIG. 4 : *Yanadi Interaction Pattern within their Worlds*

back the *yathabondi* or shadow and put it in the body of the ailing person. Figure 4 provides the interaction pattern of the Yanadi, non-Yanadi, gods, devils, plants and animals in the visible and invisible world. The essential elements of the

Yanadi world view are :

1. The dichotomous categorization of the universe into visible and invisible and benign and malign;
2. Simultaneous inhabitation of the Yanadi in two distinct worlds ;
3. Superiority of the non-Yanadi, gods and devils to Yanadi;
4. Helpful nature of benign non-Yanadi and gods who always help the Yanadi but at the same time chide them;
5. Maintaining harmony with the inhabitants of both worlds by subjugation.

Spatial arrangements of Yanadi living

The largest landmass conceived by the Yanadi is Sriharikota island. However, a person is identified with the village or habitation (*ooru*) in which he lives. Each *ooru* has a name and generally refers to a non-Yanadi village. The *ooru* is essentially a non-Yanadi village indicating sedentary living. If the Yanadi is living near a *ooru* he identifies his habitation with the non-Yanadi *ooru.* A Yanadi habitation is referred to by the Yanadi as *ma indlu* (our houses). The non-Yanadi call the Yanadi habitation simply as *yanadolla gudiselu* (huts of the Yanadi) simply and not as an *ooru* of the Yanadi. This distinction also reflects the differences between the sedentary non-Yanadi living and the nomadic Yanadi living. When there is work at a distant place, for a short period, the Yanadi erect temporary huts, complete the work and return to the *ooru.* Such temporary habitations are referred to as *adavalu.*

In each Yanadi habitation, there would be a few clusters of huts. Each cluster generally consists of the huts (*indlu* or *gudiselu*) of a person, his married sons and daughters. When he has no married sons and daughters, he would be living in the cluster of huts of his brother or sister. Each cluster hut maintains some distance from another cluster hut. The Yanadi habitation pattern is a concrete manifestation of his world view in which huts of the elders are located in the south and west which are high (*eguva*). Similarly the huts of younger persons are located in north and east side at a lower place (*digva*). The habitation pattern becomes quite perceptible when the clusters of huts are situated very near to each other. The God's hut is always erected west or south of the huts of its owner which faces east.

Figure 5 provides an example of Yanadi habitation. There are four distinct clusters of huts. In each cluster the oldest Yanadi lives either south or west of the cluster. A majority of these clusters belong to one *intiperu*. God's hut is erected

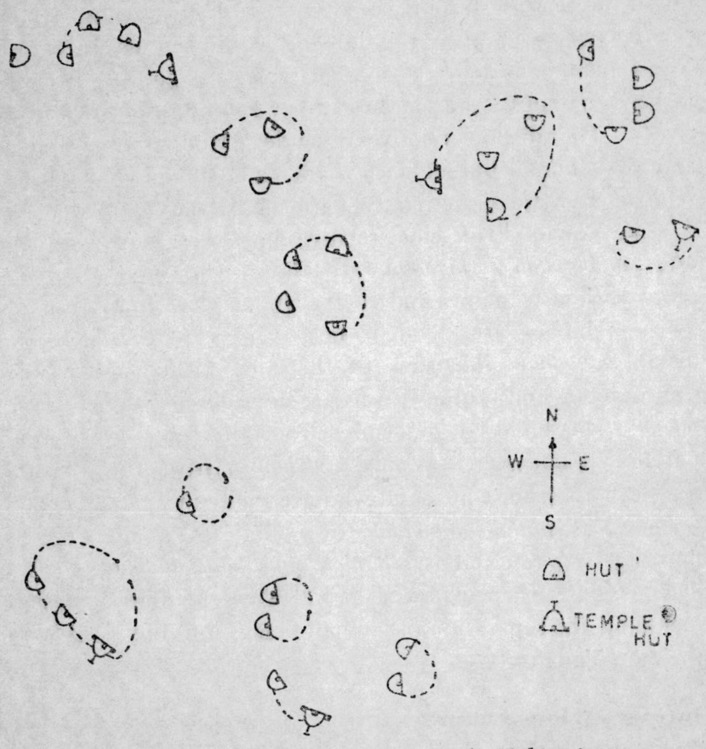

FIG. 5 : *Notional Map of a Yanadi Habitation*

south or west of the hut of its owner. The habitation is on an elevated ground surrounded by jungle.

Yanadi human relationships

The Yanadi broadly group all human beings into Yanadi and non-Yanadi and among the Yanadi into non-relatives and relatives. They term non-relatives as *mavalla manisi kani mamanisi kadu* (those who are Yanadi but not related) and relatives as *mamanisi* or *mabandulu* (my relative). A Yanadi refers to another

Yanadi as non-relative when he cannot trace the relationship. A Yanadi considers another Yanadi as his relative when he can trace the actual relationship or when he has the knowledge that he is a relative even though he may not be able to trace the actual relationship. The Yanadi recognizes another Yanadi as a distant relative when he has knowledge about the relationship but may not be able to trace it. A close relative is one whose relationship could be easily traced. The Yanadi consider grandparents, parents, mother's siblings, father's siblings, and parents in-law as important close relatives. The distant relatives include grandparents' siblings, spouse's siblings, parents-in law and their siblings. The distant relatives becomes close relatives after marriage.

The Yanadi divide close relatives into two groups : *dayadulu* and *sambandulu*. *Dayadulu* are those who have the same *intiperu* (house name) and with whom they cannot marry. These relatives are divided into very close *dayadulu* and distant *dayadulu*. The sons of the same father and mother, step-parents, and brother's sons are considered very close *dayadulu*. The children descended from the same great-grandparents are considered as only *dayadulu*. The mother's brother and father's sister's husband who are related by blood are referred to as *sontha sambandulu* (own affinals). Yanadi related by marriage are referred as *pillanichchina badesthulu* or *sambandulu*. Figure 6, provides a broad view of these divisions, including the separation of human beings into the Yanadi and the non-Yanadi.

Intiperu (House name)

The Yanadi tribe is divided into a number of exogamous *intiperus*. Twenty-seven *intiperus* are identified in Sriharikota island. A Yanadi divides all these *intiperus* into two distinct categories : one comprising those *intiperus* having descended from a common ancestor among whom marriage is prohibited and other comprising *intiperus* in which marriages are desirable and preferred. For example, a Yanadi belonging to Eegala will not marry another Eegala but must marry in the *intiperu* of Thupakula. Within the set of marriageable *intiperus*, the preferred ones are mother's brother's *intiperu*, and father's sister's husband's *intiperu*. Other *intiperu* marriages are negotiated when a preferred *intiperu* is not available.

Household

The interaction in a Yanadi household is relaxed, informal and direct. The Yanadi household consists of men, women and their unmarried children. No matter what form of marriages take place, there seems to be very little difference in the role of relationship between husband and wife. A wife does not refer to her husband by name, though the husband does. However, the sense of equality is maintained between the two. Overt verbal expression are used equally by both husband and wife. After reaching adulthood the father treats his son as an equal and exchange cigars or *beedies* or share toddy and *arrack* (liquor). As a normative behaviour, children are expected to respect their parents. Generally, all members of the household eat together. They gather near the hearth with plates after the mother announces that the food is ready for distribution. The mother distributes the food according to individual desires but more food is served for those who are working. Every member of the household has to finish the food and clean his or her own plate.

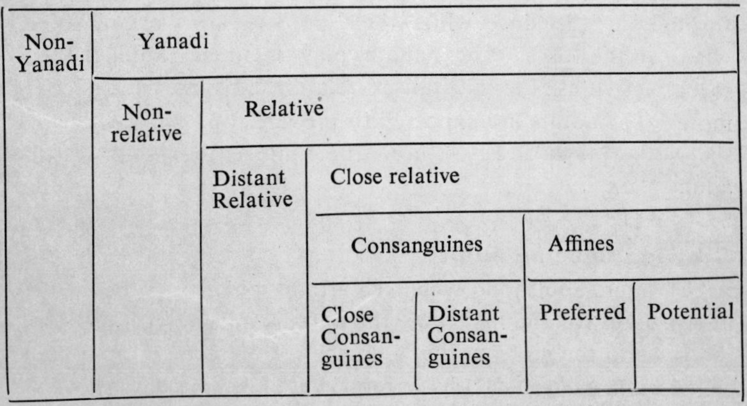

FIG. 6 : *Dichotomous Division of Yanadi Relatives*

A Yanadi household hut is a collective possession and is constructed with the help of all members. The responsibility to look after the hut and the younger siblings when the parents go to work lies with older children. Sex linked differences are observed in household activities. The older girls are expected to bring water, clean utensils, and prepare rice whereas boys of the same age are expected to collect firewood and bring fish or any other edibles from the forest for the evening meal. Grown up boys and girls remain a part of the parents' household until they set up their own households. Seldom do unmarried boys and girls live separately from their parents

Within the household, individual members enjoy freedom of work, rest and relaxation. There is little compulsion on youngsters to work. Even if a youngster fails to comply with the demands of the parents he or she is seldom punished either physically or socially. One can say that a Yanadi household provides full freedom to its members and each individual is left to live in his or her own world. Possessions like a few pieces of cloth, utensils and knives are respected very highly as these are generally purchased by the individuals from their own earnings.

There seems to be a dichotomy between the worlds of adults and children. The young children are left to play whereas adults are expected to work. It is quite common to observe the Yanadi children playing in and around the habitation throughout the day, while their parents are working somewhere in the forest. The Yanadi play includes indulgence in sexual activities. Pre-marital sex relationships are not uncommon. The adults are expected to provide food and shelter to the young regardless of how the children respond to the adults.

Growing to be an adult

A girl enters adulthood when she attains puberty. When a girl menstruates for the first time, the parents of the girl pass on the news to the girl's mother's brother. He erects a small hut called *chatu gudies* near the parents' hut. For nine days she lives in this hut and is considered impure. In the early hours of the ninth day, the *chatu gudies* is burnt by the mother's brother and in the evening the girl is bathed in hot water and provided with new clothes. She is now purified and is taken into the parents' hut. In the night of this day, *seekadimpu* ceremony is celebrated. The expenditure for this is met by collecting contributions of Rs. 5 to 10 or some amount of rice from all *dayadulu* and *sambandulu*. This money is used to purchase provisions, rice, vegetables and new clothes for the girl. An artist is engaged for singing and dancing (*malem*) during the ceremony who is paid Rs. 20 to 40 with food and liquor. The girl is married within one or two months after attaining puberty and is declared a woman.

The Yanadi consider a boy an adult, when he grows a moustache and beard. Generally, when a boy starts working as a forest worker or labourer, he is treated as an adult. It is then time for him to get married. In most cases, overt indulgence of the boy in sexual activities and his desire to have a wife is considered as an indication of adulthood. No ritual is known to be performed like those of girls as a mark of transition of a boy into adulthood.

Marriage

The Yanadi prefer to marry mother's brother's daughter or son and father's sister's daughter or son. In the absence of preferred alliance, far *sambandulu* are consulted. Arranging a marriage is considered to be the responsibility of the mother's brother. In his absence, the sister's husband and other *sambandulu* take the initiative.

Marriage among the Yanadi is a matter of individual preference. Both males and females have a say in the choice of a spouse within prescribed rules. In a majority of the unions, male relatives are involved in negotiations. Hence, the girl's consent is considered most important before finalizing a marriage. A marriage cannot take place against the will and wishes of a girl and if a marriage ceremony is performed against the wishes of a girl it cannot last long.

Broadly, the Yanadi marriages are of two types. In the first form, a marriage is arranged and negotiated collectively between the relatives, specially the mother's brothers (if alive). Such marriages are referred to as *pendli* or *vivaham*. The second form of marriage is based on individual choice, with or without the approval of relatives and is referred to as *kalusukodam*. A majority of the Yanadi perform *pendli* when they get married for the first time, whereas a large number of re-marriages are of the second type. In both forms of marriage the Yanadi attach very little importance to rituals and ceremonies.

The husband expects his wife to work along with him, cook food, keep hot water in the evening for bath, sleep with him, keep clean the surroundings of the hut, use money and provisions judiciously, and look after him when he falls sick. The wife expects her husband to earn a sufficient livelihood, provide her with clothing, not to scold her or beat her, sleep with her, and avoid talking to other young women especially with potential mates. The girl's parents expect that the son-in-law should help them at times of scarcity of food and give them money when they need. The groom's parents expect their daughter-in-law to give respect to them, provide them food whenever they visit and talk to them pleasingly. Continued breach of the above norms leads to separation. Separation is a very simple affair among the Yanadi. Normally, the wife initiates the process. Generally the wife goes to her father's hut or the husband goes to his parents' or brother's sister's hut if he is staying with the girl's parents. After separation or death of the spouse, the survivor, irrespective of age, can find another partner to live with.

Pregnancy and birth

The Yanadi wish that marriage should be followed by the birth of a child. Children are considered as an asset and desirable. They believe that semen discharged by man accumulates in the womb of woman and forms into a baby when Brahma puts life into it. Pregnancy is recognized by the cessation of mensus, giddiness and increased liking for sour eatables. The pregnant woman continues to work until it becomes difficult for her. At the time of delivery, the woman stays in her hut. The delivery takes place with the help of women from neighbouring huts, usually, husband's mother and husband's brothers' wives. Generally, the woman delivers in sitting position. The mother remains confined to the hut for nine days after delivery. During this period she is served with diet cooked by an old relative who had helped in the delivery. *Purudu* ceremony is performed in the evening of the ninth day to show their gratitude to gods for safe delivery and to request *Gangaamma* to protect the mother and the child from post-natal complications.

The child is breast-fed until it voluntarily withdraws from it. The mother takes great care of the child until it starts walking. When the child is able to walk, it is left in the company of other older children. It is believed that children acquire skill and knowledge by imitation. The Yanadi also believe that children inherit the behavioural characteristics of their parents.

Death

The news of death is circulated by a *dayadi* and a *sambandi*. Carrying a stick is the symbol of news of death. They inform all the relatives in different settlements. The *sambandi* of the dead man informs the news to his *sambandi*. At that time the *dayadi* should not speak. Food is not prepared in any hut, till the dead body is taken away. The main affinal relatives (mother's brother) supervise the burial and post-funeral ceremonies. The dead body is carried by four persons, preferably by two *sambandulu* and two *dayadulu*.

Two *sambandulu* dig a grave chest-high of three feet breadth. The ditch faces the north. The dead body is placed in a prostrate position, the face facing east. The ditch is filled with sand. A pot of water is kept at the side of the head.

The Yanadi conduct two ceremonies after the death. They are *paluposukovadam* and *punyaham* for children and *karamanthralu* for married adults. When a person dies, the *dayadulu* of that person become impure (*antudarlu*). After conducting *punyaham* or *karmanthralu* they are purified.

Rituals and festivals

Yanadi mainly celebrate Sankranti; other festivals of the non-Yanadi like Sivaratri and Deepavali are also celebrated. They also conduct *devudi karyam* (worship of god festival) to please the gods in gratitude for solving some of their problems. It is conducted on any convenient day. The *ambali posedi* ritual is conducted after all persons in a habitation have recovered from epidemic diseases. This is to give a revered send-off to gods who visited them, since it is believed that epidemic diseases are caused by gods.

4

Shrinking Yanadi World

YANADI have been depending entirely on the visible world (*naralokam*) either directly or indirectly for their survival in the forest. The dependency is so high that the Yanadi think themselves as part and parcel of it. When the Yanadi are asked whether they knew any thing of the life outside the island or about non-Yanadi they would reply, "How do we know all those things? We have been roaming and living in the forest. If you ask us about the plants, leaves and animals in the island, we can tell you". This clearly reflects the Yanadi's close association with the forest.

Yanadi and the forest

The Yanadi's direct contact with nature was broken with the arrival of the British. The British employed them to collect chay roots and jungle produce; in turn they were provided with clothes, cigars, and rice. Cash economy was introduced in the life of the Yanadi. But the Yanadi depended largely on non-saleable forest food. The British were sympathetic towards the Yanadi. The relations between the British and the Yanadi were one of harmonious co-existence. However, the British looked down upon the Yanadi as savage human beings, while the Yanadi accepted British superiority.

The arrival of the British brought the Yanadi in touch with the local non-Yanadi which resulted in some changes in the Yanadi life style. The non-Yanadi villagers sold Yanadi country liquor, provisions, clothes, axes and knives to the Yanadi. Some of the Yanadi were employed by the forest contractors in cutting and loading wood. A few remained with the forest officials to do forest works. Thus, Yanadi dependence on the forest was partially reduced. This process continued till ISRO took over the island in 1970. Even in 1976, it was observed that the forest served as the source of food, house construction and medicine.

Forest provides food

Among the fruits and roots of edible plants, the Yanadi eat *yallagaddalu* (Stamen tubers) and palmyrah (*Borassus flabellofer*) in large quantities. *Yallagaddalu* creepers grow throughout the island. The plant produces a bundle of tubers from a few centimetres to 50 to 60 centimetres in length and two to five centimetres thickness. The ground is dug with a *thanga* (a kind of axe having a rectangular blade fixed to a 20 to 30 centimetres long wooden shaft) wherever the root has penetrated. The small branches and roots of the host plant are cut with a *vankathi* (a curved thick iron metallic blade fixed to a 20 to 30 centimetres handle). The tubers are collected in a basket made of palmyrah leaves. During winter and early summer, it is a common sight to see old Yanadi and older children, returning to their huts in the evening with basketfuls of tubers. Raw fruits of the palmyrah are cut and the kernels are eaten. The fruits are collected, slightly roasted and eaten. The seeds are buried which give rise to seedlings. The seedlings are either boiled or roasted on fire. Before the monsoon, every Yanadi habitation would be filled with palmyrah fruit odour. Again after the monsoon, in the morning and evening, one observes Yanadi enjoying the palmyrah seedlings. Less frequently consumed tubers are *donda gaddalu, gotichikkudu gaddalu, eesiti gaddalu, damaragaddalu, gitti gaddalu* (*Pbeospormum spinosum*) which are found in ponds and streams. Yanadi consume the fruits such as *neredu* (*Elaeodendrum glaucum*), *alli* (*Memecylon umbellatum*), *regu* (*Zyziphus mauritiana*), *purudu* (*Fluggea species*), *eetha* (*Phoenix sylvestris*), *beera* (*Hugonia mytax*), *donda* (*Coccinia indica*) and *parika* (*Zyziphus ochophlia*). Generally women and children collect these fruits on their way home from work or when they go to collect firewood. These fruits are eaten in small quantities. The Yanadi also eat the seeds of *thamba* (*Canavalia species*), *guriginja* (*Abrus pricatorius*), and *chinthaku* (*Tamarindus indica*), but on very rare occasions. During monsoon, fresh leaves of *kuraku, isakadasaraku, chinthaku* (*Tamarindus indica*), *boddeku ponnagantiaku, munagaaku*

(*Moriga oloifera*), and *chenchalliaku* are consumed.

The forests contain not only salubrious food but also several poisonous tubers such as *nageti gaddalu* and *ganneru* (*Nerium odorum*), leaves and flowers. The Yanadi avoid these poisonous tubers.

Another important forest food the Yanadi relish is honey. According to the Yanadi, there are four types of honey : *thorra thene* (furrow honey), *musari thene* (flocking honey), *kommu thene* (branch honey) and *pulla thene* (stick honey). *Thorra thene* is said to be the sweetest of all the four varieties. To collect the honey, smoke is produced with green leaves and is brought to the honeycomb. The bees fly away by the smoke, leaving the comb. Then the comb is plucked. In the case of *musari thene* leaves of the *gonji* tree (*Glycosmis mauritiana*) are chewed and blown into the furrow of the tree where honey-bees flock. By the smell of the leaves, the bees fly away. When the bees leave the comb, the honey is collected. The Yanadi give honey to young children. It is believed that honey enables the children to talk early and speak clearly. Honey is also used to treat burns.

Fishing is one of the important food procuring activities. There are instances of the Yanadi deciding to go to fishing and foregoing a day's work. In recent days, fishing has become a hobby. The implements used for fishing are *ootha mandam* and *galem* (angler). *Ootha* is prepared by a 90 centimetre length thin bundle of dried sticks of *narudu* and *gongi* (*Glycosmis mauritiana*) trees. These are tied parallel to each other into a tumbler shape with the help of a creeper (*mulla theega*). To give the shape and strength one big cane frame circularly bent is fixed inside the thin sticks at the middle and a small circular cane frame through which a hand can be inserted at the narrow end and tied with a cane reed to the thin sticks. *Mandam* is like javelin with a 'U' shaped iron piece fixed to the thicker end of a long pole. The metal has two barbs inside of the 'U' shape. The metal is purchased from non-Yanadi and the pole is procured from the forest. The *galem* needle (angler) and nylon thread are purchased from non-Yanadi. Yanadi fish in the shallow water of streams, ponds, ditches and lakes with the help of *ootha* and *mandam* whereas the angler is used for deep water fishing using a round worm as bait. When there is little water in a ditch, the Yanadi bail out water and catch the fish with bare hands. Quite often the Yanadi adopt this method. In knee deep water Yanadi carefully watch the movements of the fish and when the fish comes close, *ootha* is immediately put over the fish and it is pressed against the ground. When the fish is trapped in the *ootha*, it is removed fromt he *ootha* from the top. For catching big fishes a *mandam* is used. First the Yanadi quietly watch the fish lying in the mud, then the *mandam* is pierced with a strong stroke on the fish, and they slowly remove the fish with the other hand from *mandam*.

The Yanadi poison the fish in rare cases with the bark or raw fruits of the *kadapa* plant. When the powder or the paste of the bark of raw fruit is mixed in the water the fish lose consciousness and float on the surface. They do not generally catch fish this way, because it kills all the fish and leaves nothing for future. The prawns in Buckingham Canal and Pulicat Lake are caught with bare hands. Crabs, tortoise and snails of the sea also form food of Yanadi. Hunting is a food procuring as well as recreational activity. They hunt rats, rabbits and varanus with the help of dogs. The Yanadi trace the hideout of the animal after identifying its footprints and disturb the animal. When the animal runs to escape, the dogs chase it. As soon as the dog catches the animal, the Yanadi relieve the animal from the dog. A variety of wild cat and mongoose are generally caught with traps. The Yanadi rarely catch birds. They are not afraid of jungle animals except a few poisonous snakes, wild boar and wild ox. One of the older Yanadi is said to be an expert snake charmer and is reported to cure snake bite. In the past, the Raithu Yanadi had hunted wild boar.

Rarely, do the Yanadi store any of the food items. The catch is just sufficient for a day or two. This may be due to ready availability of forest food. An exception is fish which the Yanadi preserve by drying and applying salt. Yanadi food gathering required only for the members of the household. So a household could easily survive without help from others. As soon as a child is able to gather food, he or she becomes an independent person. Even as wage labourers, the Yanadi remain independent. Owing to these factors, the possibilities of an independent living for the Yanadi have been very high. The freedom available in human relationships might have further fostered the independent living of the Yanadi.

Forest provides cure for diseases

The forest is also a source of some 60 medicinal plants which are used to cure many common diseases. Irrespective of sex, all adult Yanadi have knowledge of medicinal plants, but a few Yanadi have better knowledge of their applications. They do not divulge the names, rather administer the medicine themselves.

Forest provides material for huts

The forest is rich with materials required for constructing huts. The frame of the hut is made by four to five metres long twigs of eucalyptus or casuarina or *alli* (*Memecylon umbellatum*) fixed on the ground in a circle of one and half metre radius, keeping a gap of twenty to thirty centimetres between them. The twigs are bent in the centre of the circle to a man's height and the tapering ends are tied with creepers (*pala theega*). The frame is thatched with dried palmyrah leaves and creepers. A small entrance is made at the bottom through which the Yanadi crawl inside. The hut is transportable and can easily be dismantled or re-erected elsewhere.

Yanadi and non-Yanadi interaction after 1970

As described in Chapter 2, till 1970, the Sarkar Yanadi had more interaction with the state government forest officials and less with the non-Yanadi. The forest officials did not interfere in the collection of forest food by the Yanadi which was their right. The Raithu Yanadi had also close contacts with the contractors, Reddy cultivators, and other non-Yanadi. The interaction of the Raithu Yanadi with the non-Yanadi extended not only to economic spheres but also to social and religious spheres. The Raithu Yanadi completely depended on the contractors for work. Generally, the Yanadi never went to the non-Yanadi for work. Instead, contractors requested the Yanadi to work for them. The Raithu Yanadi mainly worked for the contractors but continued to collect fruits and roots, hunted animals and caught fish like the Sarkar Yanadi.

The take over of the island by ISRO brought about change. The habitat where the Yanadi were rehabilitated on the mainland would not provide them food, shelter and medicinal plants. The new non-Yanadi neighbours instead of being helpful cheated them in all possible ways. The Yanadi made all efforts to return to the island and those who were hiding in the jungle slowly joined the other Yanadi on the island.

The environment which greeted the Yanadi was not the one which they were accustomed to: new migrants with sophisticated machinery, new forest officials, new contractors and security personnel. The tubers, fruits, animals and fish were there but under the strict control of new security personnel. The Yanadi were not allowed to touch them.

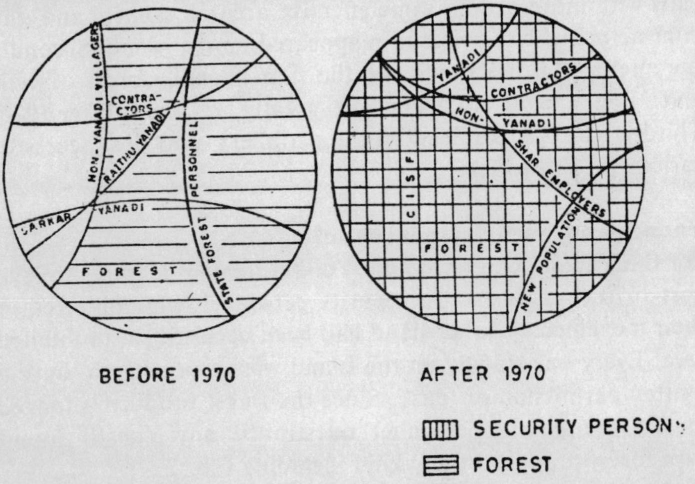

FIG. 7 : *Showing the changing pattern of interaction*

Figure 7 shows the significant changes that took place after 1970. The circle hypothetically represents the physical entity of the island. Each line represents the area in terms of 'power of control' or movement of the persons. The interaction of the lines and the area in between them represent interaction.. Four-fifths of the area was covered with forest which was controlled and maintained by the state forest department before 1970. After 1970 about half of the area is covered by forest and the remaining areas are part of SHAR's new activities and a few of non-Yanadi villages signifying their contact. Similarly the Raithu Yanadi mostly interacted with the contractors, forest officials and a few non-Yanadi villagers.

Other significant changes had taken place in the island after 1970. The Yanadi had become marginal whereas the complete island is covered by forest, security personnel, buildings, laboratories, workshops, launching pads and test pads. Now only a small portion is covered by the Forestry and Horticulture Section of SHAR administration. The Yanadi have no contact with the new population except as their employees, working in various sections of the SHAR administration.

Three salient features are noticeable. Firstly, the forest officials with more or less same effective area of control and the contractors with lesser area reappeared on the island. Secondly the interaction of Yanadi with the non-Yanadi, forest officials and non-Yanadi villagers got greatly reduced after 1970. Thirdly, the Yanadi lived on the periphery and lost access to various forest produce.

Yanadi and security personnel

For the Yanadi, one of the most disheartening features of the post-1970 changes was the security personnel who objected to their movements as the island had been declared a prohibited area. Every one staying on the island was expected to have a written permission or 'pass'. Since the forest produce belonged to ISRO, the security personnel questioned any Yanadi found with forest produce of any kind including fish.

The new situation was so disheartening for the Yanadi that they tried their best to remain out of sight of any security personnel or men whom they suspected to be connected with security. At times, a few Yanadi were spotted by the security personnel in the process of collecting fruits and fishing in the ponds. The security personnel brought these Yanadi to the security post and detained them for hours. The security personnel at first thought that the Yanadi were undesirable and illegal entrants to the island. However, the Yanadi's submissive and non-protesting behaviour made the security personnel ponder over their own actions. On occasions when the security personnel lost their patience against the perseverance and patience of the 'quiet' and 'dumb' Yanadi, they just asked the Yanadi to go away with the instruction that they should not be seen again. This made the even Yanadi more meek and submissive.

As late as 1976, anthropologists observed expression of continuated intimidation in various forms. A few Yanadi also reported that their goats and chicken were snatched away. The resultant effect was that the security personnel were classified by the Yanadi as visible, most powerful malign ghosts (*dhurthulu*). Until then, they had only known invisible malign ghosts and milder harmful non-Yanadi in the visible world. This was an extremely new and fearful experience for the Yanadi. As time passed by the presence of security personnel was felt more and more by the Yanadi.

Life had become extremely insecure for the Yanadi and they had been forced to live in a constant state of fear of being thrown out of the island. At the same time, their past experience on the mainland, at least for a few of them, was such that they wanted to remain on the island at any cost.

Yanadi and SHAR Administration

Among other things, the Raithu and Sarkar Yanadi were forced to work as daily wage casual labourers in the forest for plantation, felling trees, and other horticultural activities planned by SHAR administration after 1970. A large number of the Yandi were quickly hired by SHAR administration. Suddenly they became a part of a labour force comprising. Telugu and Tamil speaking non-Yanadi with varying religious and *jati* identities.

The presence of Telugu-speaking non-Yanadi of the island was a great respite to the Yanadi. The take over of the island brought a fundamental change in the lives of the Yanadi as they became a part of a cash economy and a large number of migrant labourers from various parts of India started competing with them. When construction work started, the Yanadis could not compete for jobs with the skilled migrant workers. Also SHAR administration found it difficult to hire Yanadis for technical jobs.

Another factor which had a profound effect on Yanadi life was maintaining a prescribed time schedule for work. To the Yanadi who were unaccustomed to the concept of punctuality, fixed hours of working and fixed holidays, the new work style was completely alien. Only the desire to stay on the island forced the Yanadi to comply with these new ways of working. Even today, it is not uncommon for most of the Yanadi to be either early or late for work. SHAR administration works for six days, Sunday being a holiday, in the first and third weeks of every month; five days' work and two days' holidays on Saturdays and Sundays during the second and fourth weeks of every month. All important national festivals are holidays most of them completely unknown to the Yanadi. This kind of work schedule further accentuated the misery of the Yanadi.

Interactions of the Yanadi with SHAR administration, were in no way comparable to their earlier experiences with the contractors or the state forest department officials where the work was generally on piece rate basis. Personnel of SHAR forestry and horticulture, and public health sections, unlike the contractors and the forest department officials, were particular about punctuality rather than the quantity and quality of work because they were employed on daily wages. So, they questioned the sincerity and honesty, and ridiculed the habits and customs of the Yanadi.

It was very difficult for the Yanadi to be punctual. They were also not permitted to collect the forest produce. Because of these constraints, a few Yanadi immediately stopped working for SHAR administration. Some of them preferred to live on forest food rather than work for SHAR administration. Some of them worked irregularly for the sake of having a written permission to stay on the island.

Many Yanadi readily worked for the contractors even on lower wages since they maintained past norms and behaviour. The Yanadi did not mind being exploited in the disguise of patronage. The Yanadi had also freedom from a tight time schedule and could collect fruits and roots from the forest from time to time.

Yanadi in vicious cycle

The restrictions on eating roots and fruits, prohibition to drink natural juice of palmyrah trees, and the introduction of cash economy made even survival very difficult. The new administrative rules and the disappearance of the barter system added further hardship to the Yanadi life. There was no one around

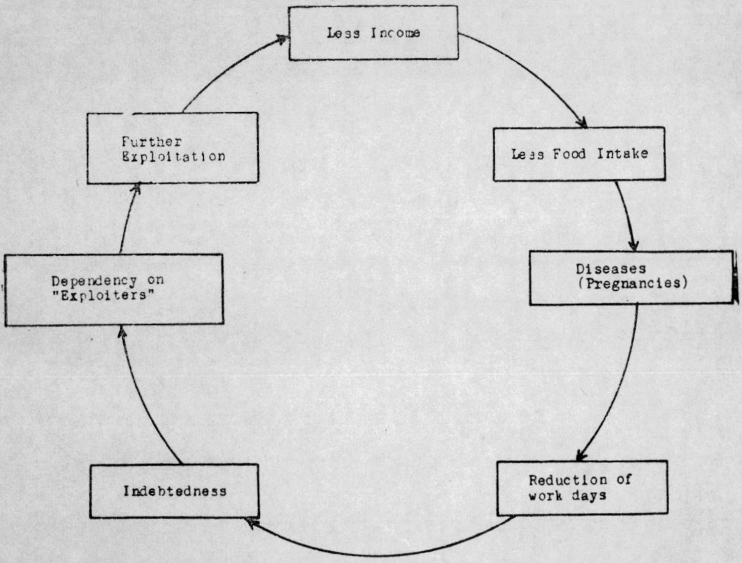

FIG. 8 : *Vicious cycle*

with whom they could exchange rice, fish, or other forest catch. None would 'advance' them food against future work. At the same time, no one except the Forestry and Horticulture section of SHAR would hire them for any work other than plantation. This void was quickly filled by a new class of 'exploiters' who came forward to help the Yanadi by giving rice on loan in the island or in Sullurpeta on credit, an inferior quality of boiled and sometimes broken rice was supplied by these exploiters. The Yanadi had no choice but to go in for credit as the total earnings were insufficient to meet their bare minimum needs. At the same time, when the Yanadi missed work or could not find work or wages were not given in time, they were totally at the mercy of these exploiters for survival. In this way, a new system of perpetual exploitation was introduced from which the Yanadi could not come out. Figure 8 shows the vicious cycle of exploitation in which the Yanadi found themselves.

The question before the anthropologists was : How is one to break this vicious circle of exploitation ?

5

Inducing Change

THE ANTHROPOLOGIST'S role after studying the culture is to identify needs and problems specific to the culture. They are prioritized for suggesting solutions. It follows developing a strategy for implementing the suggested solutions within available resources and constraints. The problems and needs of the Yanadi were studied in two phases. In the first phase, the observed needs and problems were identified with the help of extensive interviews and quick analysis. In the second phase, an intensive and detailed study was conducted to identify observed as well as felt needs in a more specific situational context (Goodenough 1963 : 64-91).

As shown in Figure 9, the needs and problems of the Yanadi were categorized in two main areas—psychological and socio-economic :

A. *Psychological Needs and Problems*

(i) Sense of insecurity
(ii) Sense of inferiority
(iii) Sense of powerlessness

B. *Socio-Economic Needs and Problems*

(i) Exploitation
(ii) Lack of education
(iii) Low earning
(iv) Lack of medical assistance
(v) Lack of leadership

In each of these two areas, specific needs and problems were identified for which concrete solutions were suggested

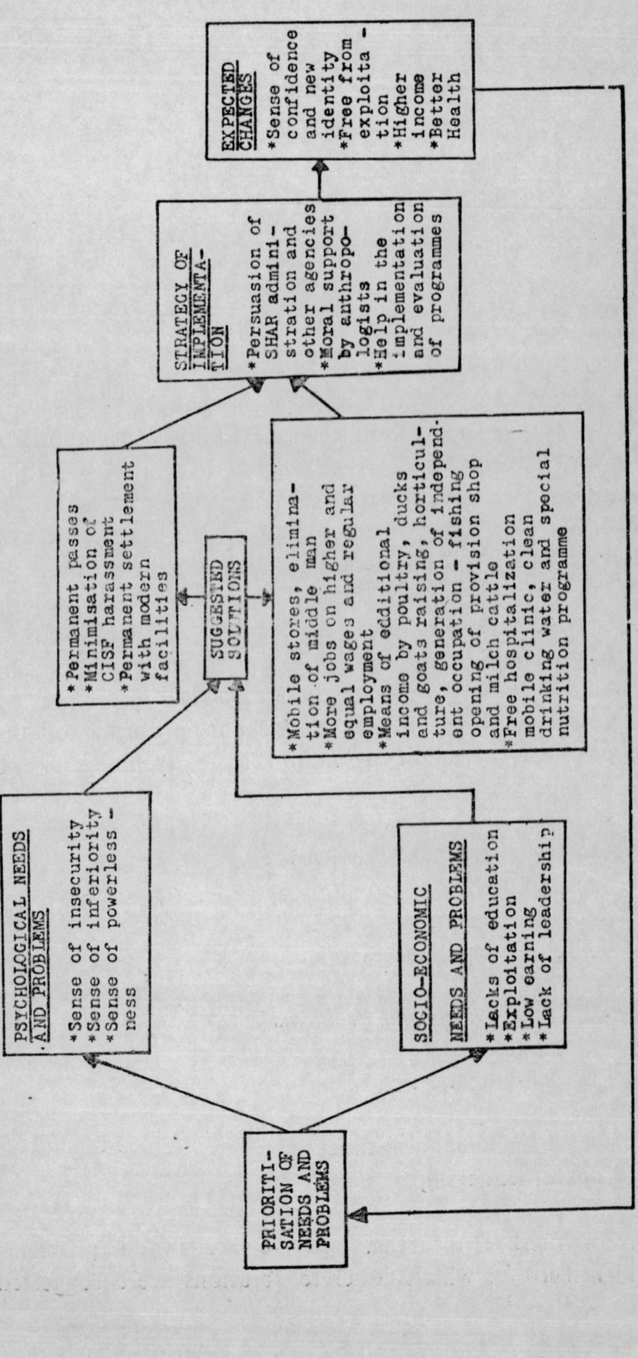

FIG. 9 : *Process of prioritization of needs and problems and introduction of change*

and the strategy of implementation was also worked out. As change agents, the anthropologists helped in implementing the suggested solutions, and monitored the changes. Mid-course corrections were also made in case those did not yield desirable results.

Psychological needs and problems

The psychological needs and problems of the Yanadi arose mainly from the conflict between the Yanadi desire to live on the island and the fear of being thrown out. After the Yanadi returned to the island, there was a perpetual struggle to stay and survive on the island. They were forced to move surreptitiously in order to avoid the security personnel. The security personnel as indicated earlier also objected to collection of forest food leading to a reduction in the availability of forest food like tubers, roots, fruits and fish to the Yanadi. The psychological effect was sense of 'powerlessness' which crept in among the Yanadis.

Furthermore, the Yanadi habitations were shifted frequently by SHAR administration according to change of work-spots. This created doubts among the Yanadi whether they would be allowed to stay on the island on regular basis. They feared that they would be chased out of the island at any time. Incompatibility in the values and expectations created further maladjustments. The Yanadi thought that SHAR administration was harsh which they could not withstand. Interference in the freedom of Yanadi movements, thought and work made them angry but they were helpless.

All these factors led the Yanadi as a group to feel insecure. The fact that they were reduced to the status of aliens on their own ancestral land has driven the entire tribe into a perennial state of anxiety. In the midst of 'powerful' and 'educated' neighbours, the Yanadi felt inferior. The alarming speed with which events took place on the island and the changes that followed made the Yanadi feel further helpless. So much was happening on the island against their wishes that they realized the futility of resisting and fighting against it.

The sum total effect on the Yanadi state of living can be characterized as a perpetual state of anxiety and a sense of helplessness. In this state, the Yanadi were most submissive and at the same time they were obsessed with a high degree of insecurity, inferiority, and powerlessness. Nothing was more important in life than means and ways which would permit them to stay on the island. We observed that this fear was the greatest obstacle and acted as a barrier between SHAR administration and the Yanadi. We have broadly defined this problem as a psychological barrier.

In the beginning of the project, on several occasions, the Yanadi gave a negative reply when suggested to grow vegetables, raise poultry and goats, reflecting all their doubts to continue on the island and the harassment of security personnel. Once in early 1978 the forest officer and an administrative officer visited Penubakam habitation and asked an old Yanadi why he did not grow some fruit-yielding trees. The old Yanadi immediately retaliated, "Why? Do you want to eat all the fruits when we grow them? It is better not to grow any." We were convinced that without creating a sense of security and permanence among the Yanadi, it would be extremely difficult to convince the Yanadi to accept any new idea. Hence, we thought to look for a solution which would help create a sense of security among the Yanadi.

To remove the psychological barrier, three solutions were suggested : (i) issue of permanent passes, (ii) minimization of the harassment of security personnel and (iii) rehabilitation of the Yanadi at permanent locations.

We thought that the issue of permanent photo-passes would help the Yanadi to think that they were being allowed by the SHAR administration to stay on the island permanently. Similarly, rehabilitation on permanent locations would drive away their constant fear of being thrown out of the island. Minimization of harassment was thought to help the Yanadi feel secure on the island. At the same time, it was argued that the first-two measures would help in reducing the harassment by the security personnel.

Without the permission of SHAR administration nobody is allowed to live or stay on the island. The employees of SHAR Centre are given permanent passes permitting them to stay on the island. The dependents of the employees and the daily wage labourers are provided with a 'temporary pass' which is

1. Yanadi dwellings *(See pages 26-27)*

2. Yanadi constructing a hut with palmyrah leaves *(See pages 38-39)*

3. Jungle fruit—the main food of the Yanadi *(See pages 11-12)*

4. SHAR Administration and the Yanadi *(See pages 40-41)*

valid for a limited period. The permanent pass holders are allowed to move anywhere on the island, but the temporary pass holders are allowed to move only within a specified area.

Those Yanadi who had been working with SHAR administration were given temporary passes. This did not make them feel comfortable because they were not supposed to enter the forest and collect forest food which was essential for their survival. Their dependents had no pass of any kind. So, all their movements were stealthy. At the same time, the passes were withdrawn as and when there was no work for the Yanadi on the island and such persons were generally forced to leave the island by the security personnel.

We felt that the Yanadi should be provided with permanent passes to generate a sense of security among them. It would restore their freedom at least partially and the Yanadi would feel free to move on the island to procure food. This would minimize the conflict between the Yanadi and the security personnel who had been harassing them. It would also help SHAR administration to keep a regular record of all the Yanadi on the island.

A high level decision of ISRO authorities was required to accomplish this goal. In a meeting with the Chairman, ISRO in July 1976, the anthropologists explained the need for permanent passes for the Yanadi. The Chairman was convinced and agreed to issue permanent photo passes to the Yanadi. However, it was not possible to initiate the work immediately. In March 1977 the anthropologists met the Controller, SHAR Centre and requested him to arrange for permanent passes as early as possible as agreed by the Chairman ISRO nine months earlier. In the first phase of this action, photos were to be taken. The Controller assigned the work of taking photographs to the Photography Section, SHAR Centre, in coordination with the Forestry and Horticulture Section, and the anthropologists. This work was started in May 1977. The anthropologists accompanied the photographer and helped him to identify the Yanadi. Individual photographs of all adult Yanadi were taken separately, and a group photo of every household was also taken. This continued till the end of July 1977 and another six months were spent in the preparation of photographs.

Finally twenty months after the initial decision about 210 Yanadi who were working with SHAR administration as daily wage labourers were issued individual permanent passes in February 1978. But their dependents and those working with the contractors were not issued such passes. However, they also required permanent passes to stay on the island. This lacuna had been brought to the attention of SHAR administration. As anticipated, the permanent passes created a sense of confidence and security among the Yanadi and removed their fear of being thrown out of the island. It also helped in reducing the harassment of security personnel to a great extent. Passes became a very valuable possession for the Yanadi. Its importance was very evident as non-pass holders have been repeatedly requesting the anthropologists for getting permanent passes issued to them. This symbolic, but very important administrative measure allowed for the first time the Yanadi a right to live on the island without fear.

Reduction of security personnel harassment

The anthropologists tried to reduce harassment by the security personnel by bringing incidents of harassments to the notice of higher authorities of SHAR administration. The Assistant Commandant, Central Industrial Security Force, was briefed from time to time by the anthropologists. SHAR administration instructed the security officials not to check passes of the residents of the Yanadi habitations without their prior permission. At the same time, issuance of permanent passes to the Yanadi made the security personnel realize that the Yanadi, henceforth, would enjoy a similar status as those of other SHAR employees. This realization gradually reduced the harassment of Yanadi by the security personnel.

Permanent settlement

Sedentary living of the Yanadi at some places was thought to be most essential for their socio-economic development. Initially, it was also thought that it would help SHAR administration to extend various amenities and facilities to the Yanadi and it would keep them out of the danger zone of the rocket launching pads. The latter analysis indicated that permanent settlement would create an atmosphere of security and feeling of continual stay on the island. According to the proposal of anthropologists, the permanent settlement of the Yanadi on the island required a policy decision and a careful analysis of the location vis-a-vis the technical plan of land utilization by SHAR Centre.

The proposal of permanent settlement was accepted in principle by the Chairman, ISRO in July 1976. Further, he suggested that SHAR administration in consultation with the anthropologists should suggest some locations. The Controller, SHAR Centre, appointed a committee to suggest a few places. The committee suggested five locations. But before the proposed plan could be finalized, SHAR administration had to reconsider the proposal in the light of fresh technical needs for declaring certain specified areas as danger zone on the island. So a fresh search for the locations began in July 1977. Accordingly, members of the Committee consulted the anthropologists, and a few Yanadi on selection of new locations. The criteria in the selection of new locations were proximity to workspots and the forest. The committee decided that Pitcharigunta, Karnalapalem and Keepakam would be settled at Kilividu whereas Kalavagu and Penubakam would be settled at Kodaledu, and B.N. Road camp will remain where it was to Solladaruvu and Maulam camps had already shifted before August 1977.

The Yanadi of Pitcharigunta, Keepakam and Karnalapalem were happy about the suggested location of Kilividu. But most of the Yanadi of Kalavagu and Penubakam were very unhappy about the proposed location of Kodaledu. Their objection was that Kodaledu was near one of the campus of the security personnel and that it was small to accommodate all the Yanadi of Penubakam and Kalavagu. The anthropologists were on to selecting another location with the help of the Yanadi. After surveying a few places, they selected Kakedurudibba, popularly known as Penubakam.

In September 1977, the Director, the Controller and other SHAR officials, and the anthropologists inspected the locations of the proposed sites. It was pointed out that Kilividu (proposed site) fell within the danger zone. So it was rejected and an alternate site Kothachenu was decided. The suggestion of the anthropologists for Kakedurudibba (Penubakam) as second site instead of Kodaledu was accepted. Therefore, it was thought to have three habitations : Kothachenu, Kakedurudibba and B.N. Road. But in January 1978, due to security reasons, it was decided to shift B.N. Road (which included Maulam and Solladaruvu) to Kakedurudibba. Thus, the eight Yanadi camps were rehabilitated in two permanent habitations—Kothachenu and Penubakam (Kakedurudibba).

Site selection for permanent settlement no doubt was an important milestone but the problems that followed in recreating a Yanadi habitation were much more difficult. It required cultural insights and a detailed understanding of the Yanadi world view as described in Chapter 3. The problem was further complicated by inadvertent but sympathetic support provided by SHAR administration.

After the selection of the site, SHAR administration came in full swing and quickly drew a layout plan for the "Yanadi Labour Camp" which included, hut sites, electrification and roads. It was a typical "mass housing" layout in which house sites, located on either side of the road, faced each other. The plan envisaged a plot of 4 m$\times$4 m for each household. This plan was drawn ignoring the anthropologists' suggestion of a 6 m$\times$6 m plot for each household. Also the Yanadi were not consulted.

As indicated in Chapter 3, a Yanadi habitation, no matter how small or big, reflects manifestation of the Yanadi world view in which huts of elders are located in south and west directions, huts of the younger persons are located in east and north, and the God's hut is always erected in south or west of its owner which faces east. At the same time no two huts will have openings facing each other.

The anthropologists helped the Yanadi to replicate this habitation pattern even within the limited space provided by SHAR administration. Once the layout was drawn the anthropologists left all the decisions about hut sites, entrance of the hut and location of the God's hut to the Yanadi. This actually helped Yanadi, in spite of very limited space to re-create a Yanadi habitation of larger population which they had not experienced in the past.

The shifting took place in March 1978. The residents of B.N. Road, Kalavagu and old Penubakam were shifted to the present Penubakam habitation and the Yanadi of Pitchari-gunta, Karnalapalem and Keepakam were shifted to Kotha-chenu habitation. SHAR administration provided trucks for the transportation of men and material to the new locations. In due course of time, other facilities were also provided like approach road, water facilities, street light and community television. The two permanent habitations are connected to the main road by permanent roads. But the Yanadi do not use them. Instead they walk either by the side of the road or use shortcuts. The Yanadi feel that the roads are hard (they do not use foot-wear) and prefer to walk on the sand which they find smooth. These roads are used by officials who visit the habitations in vehicles.

Water facilities, street lights and TV

Five handpumps at Penubakam and seven at Kothachenu were installed. In each habitation two wells were also dug. Detailed analysis of its effects will be presented in Chapter 9.

Electric street lights were provided to Kothachenu in May 1978 and at Penubakam in July 1978 by giving temporary con-nection. It was for the first time that the Yanadi of Srihar-ikota were to live in a habitation with street lights. But in April 1979, temporary connection was disconnected to mini-mize electrocution. The anthropologists discussed the matter with the Assistant Administrative Officer (in-charge of labour welfare) and the Controller. The Controller assured them that permanent electric connections would soon be provided. In early 1980, at Kothachenu underground cables were laid and the power supply was resumed. This could not be done soon as the distance from the power supply point and habitation was very close whereas in Penubakam the distance is about 1.5 kilo-metres requiring large investment. Still the Controller, infor-med the anthropologists that efforts were being made to provide street lights to Penubakam. In July 1980, the Controller sug-gested a temporary solution of street lighting by providing kero-sene street lamps which were available with security personnel. The cost of kerosene would have to be met from the Yanadi Welfare Fund. Accordingly, eight lamps and seventeen litres of kerosene were procured and provided on August 9, 1980 by the anthropologists. One Yanadi was put incharge and he was instructed and explained how to light the lamp and clean the lamp everyday. Due to non-availability of kerosene, the street lamps were lit only for three weeks. These lamps provided some lighting for moving around in the habitation.

Absence of street lights has opened the roads to jackals and snakes. One may ask whether these creatures entered the Yanadi camps when they were living in darkness. The answer is that after permanent settlement the Yanadi started rearing poultry, ducks, and goats. The jackals who have multiplied many fold in the absence of their predators, have started coming to Yanadi habitations to snatch away the poultry and kids. The Yanadi believe that the snakes come to eat the excreta of poultry and eggs or chicks. We will analyse these problems in detail in Chapter 7.

Street lighting has brought a few changes in the behaviour of the Yanadi. Many believe that malign activities of many ghosts in the nights have reduced because of street lights. The observable effects was that the Yanadi children began to play under the lights. The Yanadi with a sense of security moved within the habitation at nights. Jackals stopped coming into the habitations. In the past, Yanadi ate and slept just after sunset. But now, a few Yanadi households start cooking food even after sunset. It has also become convenient for the Yanadi women to fetch water and cook food before dawn. Movements in the habitation have increased, especially among the children. It was also observed that, after the evening meal, the Yanadi gossip for an hour or so under the street lights. This was a major departure from the life style of the Yanadi who had earlier used firewood for lighting.

In permanent habitations, community television sets were installed in October 1978. When the temporary power connection was disconnected TV sets stopped functioning. In the cyclonic storm of 1979 the antennae of both sets were damaged. They are yet to be repaired. Television programmes start at 6.30 p.m. and continue till 10.30 p.m. Irrespective of age and sex the Yanadi assembled to view the programme. The Yanadi did not understand the TV programmes as the programmes were in the Tamil language. However, they liked movies (irrespective of language) and folk music. During news, and lectures of any kind, the Yanadi went to the toilet, others smoked beedies. Television brought change in Yanadi sleeping habits. Those who viewed TV went to sleep much later. On Saturdays and Sundays, when movies were telecast 50 to 60 Yanadi at Penubakam and 35 to 40 Yanadi at Kothachenu viewed it till 10.30 p.m. On other days, they watched TV till 8.30 p.m. or so and then retired. The Yanadi could learn a few Tamil words like *vanakkam* (greetings) owing to TV viewing.

Three important lessons were learnt in the process of implementing the permanent settlement for the Yanadi. Firstly, the idea of permanent settlement stemmed as a result of the Yanadi's constant fear of being thrown out of the island. The semi-nomadic Yanadi accepted the idea of sedentary living because they thought it would provide them permanent living on the island and at the same time it would restore their freedom to move on the island for procuring forest food. The anthropologists reached the same conclusion, but with a different reasoning. The anthropologists argued that once the Yanadi are settled in a specific locale it would be feasible and possible to induce changes in the Yanadi life. For SHAR administration permanent settlement provided better supervision and control over the Yanadi. It also meant more efficient implementation of the anthropologists' suggestions. In spite of the different interests, the goal could be achieved because the Yanadi, the anthropologists and the SHAR administration each had some positive things to gain at the end. Secondly, at the time of actual resettlement, a great amount of perceptional differences were observed between SHAR administration and the Yanadi desire for living in a particular way. Understanding of the Yanadi world view and their spatial arrangements of living, helped the resettlement without any serious conflict or confrontation. Lack of such an understanding might have led to the abandoning of the idea of providing a sedentary living for the semi-nomadic Yanadi. Probably the Yanadi would have been accused of being 'irrational' in accepting the 'progressive idea' which was beneficial to them. Thirdly, our observations indicate that the Yanadi have shown remarkable adaptive ability. It is because even in the sedentary living, they continue to enjoy the freedom of a semi-nomadic style of living. At the same time, they had very little to choose between being thrown out of the island or living close to each other with freedom. In the Yanadi view, the alternative was to be either of the two or none at all. Hence, they preferred the second alternative which was further augmented with their say in the selection of the site and some choice in the settlement plan.

Problem of exploitation

The most important recurring problem has been that of exploitation of the Yanadi by the non-Yanadi. Historical data provide unmistakable evidence of continuous exploitation of the Yanadi by contractors, forest officials, farmers, and later shopkeepers. The means, quality and magnitude of exploitation might have differed at different times but essentially the forces of exploitation reduced the Yanadi to sub-human levels. Each non-Yanadi who interacted with the Yanadi, tried to earn more than his due share. This was done by using the rules of market economy with the Yanadi who understood only the barter system.

The contractors paid very little while getting a large quantum of work done by the Yanadi. Earlier the forest officials had exploited the Yanadi by manipulating muster-rolls, collecting free honey, fish, and other forest produce, and giving petty loans, which have not ended even today. The farmers paid low wages and asked the Yanadi to work for long hours. More recently came the shopkeepers and money-lenders. The Yanadi's rupee could not fetch the same quality and quantity of rice for them as it could for the non-Yanadi. In the name of mercy and help, bad quality of rice, that too less than the professed weight, was supplied to the Yanadi on credit on which sometimes high interest was charged. In sum total, the effect of these exploitative forces reduced the Yanadi into a perpetual state of sub-human living without any respite and relief. As the time passed by, the hands of the exploiters came very close to the necks of the Yanadi.

This all-pervasive phenomenon of exploitation was so apparent and visible that assisting the Yanadi to come out of this vicious cycle became the prime aim of the anthropologists. All efforts that were contemplated were singularly aimed at attacking the forces of exploitation in a variety of ways. It was explicitly assumed that fulfilment of any need must contribute towards attacking the exploitative forces. Explicitly and sometimes implicitly, various new means of survival, suggested in the following chapters were geared to achieve this goal. In the changed circumstances shopkeepers and contractors ranked the highest in the list of exploitators.

Exploitation by shopkeepers

Topping the list of exploiters are shopkeepers. Analysis of the Yanadi life style indicated that they had suddenly changed from barter economy to cash economy. Since a majority of them were illiterate, they hardly knew simple calculations. Thus, the Yanadi would enter the shops of Sullurpeta without knowing the exact amount and prices of various produces. The glib shopkeepers would grab the money of the Yanadi and provide inferior provisions. The Yanadi could never know what he was expected to for the amount paid. When the Yanadi did not go to work due to sickness and other eventualities, the wily shopkeepers showed pity and offered provisions on credit. Enticed by the credit, the Yanadi would buy provisions at high prices. Later when the Yanadi came with their wages, they gave it to shopkeepers towards repayment of earlier credit and brought provisions on fresh credit. Thus began a cycle which had no end.

The Yanadi had to go mainly to Sullurpeta for buying provisions since there were no shops in their habitations. In the process they had to incur an extra expenditure of Rs. 2 towards transportation from their meagre income. Also, they had to walk several kilometres to catch a bus. The anthropologists brought the problem of exploitation and difficulties in visiting Sullurpeta for purchase of provisions to the attention of the Controller. They requested him to provide shopping facilities at some of the habitations or to provide transportation facility to Yanadi on weekends to visit Sullurpeta for this purpose. As a result of a meeting between Controller and the anthropologists it was decided to run a mobile provision store. For the time being, the anthropologists accepted the idea. But they thought of exploring the possibilities of Yanadi-run shops.

Mobile provision stores

The objective of running mobile provision stores was to provide provisions at fair prices as well as to acquaint the Yanadi gradually with the formal market system. From March 1977, the mobile provision store started visiting the roadside Yanadi habitations at B.N. Road and Pitcharigunta every Sunday. Even after the permanent settlement, the mobile provision store continues to visit the two habitations.

In the beginning, the response was not encouraging. Most of the Yanadi were in debt and their weekly earnings were not sufficient to buy provisions for one week. They feared that the shopkeepers would not give them credit if they stopped buying regularly from them. Moreover, the weekly trips to purchase provisions provided them with an opportunity to taste drinks which they like most.

The Yanadi also had some misapprehensions regarding the price and quantity of rice while buying from a mobile store. In the market, the Yanadi brought rice in measures, while in the mobile store, it was sold by weight. The Yanadi thought that rice sold by weight would mean a lesser quantity for the same price. It was observed that they were more concerned about quantity rather than quality. The anthropologists, therefore, brought a measuring pot from one of the Yanadi huts and weighed a kilogram of rice purchased at the mobile store. This was transferred to the measuring pot and it was full. This was sufficient to dispel their misapprehensions about quantity.

A few Yanadi were still buying rice from shopkeepers at Rs. 2.25 a kilogram when it was Rs. 2.00 in the mobile store. It was explained to the Yanadi that prices at the mobile store were lower than those at the shops. Some Yanadi at B.N. Road realized that prices at the mobile store were reasonable and started buying their provisions from there. Within eight months of operations of the mobile store, many of the Yanadi were able to pay off their debts.

It was observed that sales at the mobile store increased gradually and were very high between October 1977 and February 1978. Investigations revealed that, in this period, water level in Buckingham Canal and Pulicat Lake rose high. Therefore, it had become difficult for the Yanadi to cross the lake. So the Yanadi at the B.N. Road settlement could not go over to Thotakatla and Pernadu villages to buy provisions. So they had to make their purchases from the mobile store. It was also observed that after the permanent settlement in March 1978, the sales of the mobile provisions store started declining gradually. It was mainly due to the Yanadi of Penubakam going to outside villages for buying provisions as they were close to them now.

The following are some of the important reasons for non-participation of the Yanadi in the mobile store programme :

(i) The Yanadi got weekly wages either on Friday or Saturday but the mobile store came on Sunday. So, they had to wait for one or two days. Some of the Yanadi were thus forced to go out of the island.

(ii) The mobile store could not supply betel leaves, nuts, incense, and fruits, like banana, used in worship.

(iii) The Yanadi use mostly low quality boiled rice. The mobile store could not procure such a kind of rice and even if they were able to get boiled rice, it was of good quality. This meant that the Yanadi had to contend with a small quantity of rice.

(iv) The mobile store now and then either forgot to bring some of the items or bought less quantity of them. The Yanadi were thus forced to go outside the island to buy just one item.

The anthropologists have been bringing these irregularities to the notice of SHAR administrators. In spite of these difficulties the mobile store came as a relief to the Yanadi during the monsoon, when it was difficult to move out of the island to buy provisions. In addition, it gave them a kind of schooling market economy.

In order to serve them better as well as to quicken the process of acclimatization, one of the anthropologists started selling rice at Pitcharigunta habitation to get the Yanadi out of debt, to make them understand market dealings and to persuade them to buy provisions from the mobile store. Yet another objective was to indirectly pressurize them to attend work regularly because rice was supplied to them only for the days they worked. The sale of rice started in September 1977.

Rice was brought from Sullurpeta by the anthropologists in private trucks plying through Pitcharigunta. In order to remove misapprehensions of profit motive and cheating, one of the local Yanadi was requested to accompany the anthropologists to Sullurpeta on each occasion. The price of rice was fixed on the basis of actual price plus transport charges.

It was assumed that the Yanadi households would purchase rice from the anthropologists and the amount saved by purchasing would help them to repay the debt. Rice was sold approximately twice a week. For the first two weeks, all the Yanadi paid the full amount in cash. But in subsequent weeks, two Yanadi did not pay. One of them had fallen sick and the other's child had become sick. Thus, they did not go to work and lost their wages. Nevertheless they were given rice on loan much against the desire of the anthropologists not to sell on credit. In the following week another Yanadi lost his pass and thus he could not work for a couple of weeks. His pregnant wife and youngest son fell ill. To him also, the rice was sold on credit. In the entire month only six households made full payment regularly, five households paid partially and three did not pay. Those who purchased rice on cash could return a debt of Rs. 142 to the shopkeepers but the Yanadi's debt with the anthropologists amounted to Rs. 400. However, eight Yanadi paid Rs. 150 after the termination of the programme from October 1977. The anthropologists incurred a loss of nearly Rs. 250. An important lesson from this effort is that at least two persons in a five-member household have to work for six days a week regularly to keep the household members above starvation level. Ill health aggravates the situation and compels the Yanadi to go for credit.

Further analysis showed that in order to repay any debt per capita income per week should be more than Rs. 5. On an average, the Yanadi household of five members borrowed provisions worth Rs. 20 a week. When two persons in a household were working, they could earn approximately Rs. 35 per week. The per capita income in a week of the household was Rs. 7. This household spent nearly Rs. 30 on diet effecting a saving of Rs. 5 a week and thus could pay off a debt of Rs. 20 per month. Similarly a three working members household earned nearly Rs. 50 a week and incurred Rs. 40 on food items and they repay the debt of Rs. 20 after two weeks.

Engaging Yanadi as contractors for collection of cashew and soapnuts

The Yanadi play a vital role in forest exploitation who in turn were exploited by the contractors. The anthropologists observed that contractors played the role of middle-men and derived great benefits from the hard labour of the Yanadi. SHAR administration had also reached the same conclusion but due to lack of permanent positions in the Forestry and Horticulture Section, they opted for daily wage labourers. Prevailing labour laws further complicated the issue as forest labourers (mostly non-Yanadi) demanded regular jobs after working for a certain period. Thus SHAR administration was forced to get the work done through the contractors. In order to extend the benefits to the Yanadi, the SHAR Controller suggested that the Yanadi form a labour cooperative society. It was hoped that the state government or cooperative banks would extend loan and management assistance to run it. Knowing the highly individualistic life style of the Yanadi, the anthropologists were very apprehensive about the success of this venture. As there existed some kind of leadership among the Sarkar Yanadi, it was hoped that they would be able to run it on their own. An alternative to the society was to give piecemeal work to a group of Yanadi on nomination basis. In SHAR Centre, work less than the value of Rs. 5,000 could be given without calling tenders to any individual to be completed within a prescribed period. So on their own, the Forestry and Horticulture Section gave a contract of less than Rs. 5,000 on experimental basis to a Yanadi. An analysis of this programme is as follows.

For the collection of cashewnut and soapnut during 1980, the island was divided into three zones. For two zones sealed tenders were called for collection of cashewnut and soapnut separately. The third zone was given to a Yanadi by name Thupakula Gopal on nomination basis. While the contractors were given contracts for collection and sale, the Yanadi was given only a collection contract. The Yanadi contractor was expected to deliver the collected material at Beripeta which was in the operation zone of the work. The Yanadi was selected by the Forestry and Horticulture officials on the basis of "living close to the operation zone", "able to read and write Telugu" and "being a sincere worker". Before assigning this work to him, acceptance of the other Yanadi was obtained. He was well informed of his responsibilities.

A supervisor of the Forestry and Horticulture Section identified 23 Yanadi of Kothachenu habitation and one non-Yanadi. There were fifteen males and eight females. Six persons were already working in the Forestry and Horticulture Section. This group was given passes in the name of the contractor, Thupakula Gopal. A field assistant was assigned to record the individual's daily collection and maintain the acquittance of payment. The field assistant was requested to help the Yanadi though a contractor is expected to do it all by himself.

The work commenced on 21 April 1980. The Yanadi went to collect cashewnut and soapnut very early in the morning. They collected the nuts in small sack bags of their own and brought them to Beripeta. Since their income depended on the amount of collection, their children and older relatives (only in six cases) also helped them. In the beginning, they collected from nearby places. But as the days passed by, they had to go to the interiors and distant places. It was also not possible to bring the collection on their own. So, the produce was brought to a central place from where it was brought to Beripeta by jeep. As soon as the material was brought, the collection of every individual was weighed and recorded.

The Forestry and Horticulture Section officials decided to pay Re. 0.40 and 0.30 for one kilogram of cashewnut and soapnut respectively. The field assistant prepared bills for the week's collection on every Monday or Tuesday of the following week. This was verified by the supervisor and the range officer of the Forestry and Horticulture Section. Gopal had to go to the accounts office to collect the demand draft. Either the supervisor or the field assistant asked Gopal to come to office on a particular day and guided him how to encash the draft at the bank. The labourers were paid on the same day.

On an average the Yanadi worked for four days a week. A Yanadi earned about Rs. 6.30 per day which was about forty per cent more than the daily wages paid by the Forestry and Horticulture Section. Further analysis indicated that only eight persons worked for four days, four worked five days, and the rest of them worked three days or less in a week.

During nine weeks, the Yanadi collected 8,846 kilograms of cashewnut and 709 kilograms of soapnut. If the produce was sold at the existing rates nearly Rs. 55,500 could be earned from cashewnut and Rs. 3,200 from soapnut. The SHAR Centre spent only Rs. 3,700 on this contract. Had the Forestry and Horticulture Section engaged labour on daily wages nearly Rs. 5,500 would have been spent because, irrespective of the quantity a person collected, the labourer had to be paid Rs. 4.45 per day. Thus, through this method of collection, approximately Rs. 2,200 were saved.

The three contractors in the other two areas could earn approximately Rs. 13,000, Rs. 20,000 and Rs. 18,000 respectively excluding the expenditure towards wages, transportation, wages to their clerks and so on. Unlike the Forestry and Horticulture Section, the contractors paid wages by measuring the produce. They used a metal container called *muntha*, containing about 3.5 kilograms of weight. The rate of payment was not the same throughout the period of collection. As the produce was available easily in the early days, wages were less, but as the produce got reduced wages were raised. The rise of wages in the latter days lured the labourers to work hard and collect more of the produce so that they could earn more. This way, the wages paid for cashewnut by one contractor was Re. 0.50 per *muntha* initially, later raised to Re. 1.00 and Rs. 1.50. Similarly he paid Re. 0.75 per *muntha* for soapnut and later Rs. 1.50. Another contractor paid Re. 0.75 per *muntha* of soapnut stepping it up to Re. 1.00, Rs. 2.00 and finally to Rs. 5.00. The last contractor paid Rs. 1.50 per *muntha* of cashewnut throughout this period.

The responsibility of the Forest and Horticulture officials was mainly to weigh the nuts and prepare bills. Taking of the draft, encashment at the bank and paying to the labourers had to be done by Gopal with help from the assistant. Generally, the accounts officials would take two weeks to pass a bill. But the Head, Forestry and Horticulture Section took special interest and requested the concerned officials to pass the bills every week. This had to be done because Gopal did not have any capital to run the project. Except on one occasion when the Head of the Forestry and Horticulture Section was on leave, all payments were made regularly. It may be observed from the above description that Gopal was a contractor just for name's sake and all the chores were done by the forest officials.

The Yanadi expressed their satisfaction with this kind of work as they were free to work whenever they liked and they were also free from the constraints of punctuality and supervision. At the same time their work was facilitated by providing transport. All the members of these households could participate in the work and wages were more than they could have earned in the Forestry and Horticulture Section. All this leads us to the conclusion that if the 'middle-men' are eliminated, Yanadi could certainly earn more. At the same time, it would be beneficial to SHAR administration. In order to achieve this goal, the involvement of Forest and Horticulture officials is essential, and some kind of training for Yanadi would also be necessary.

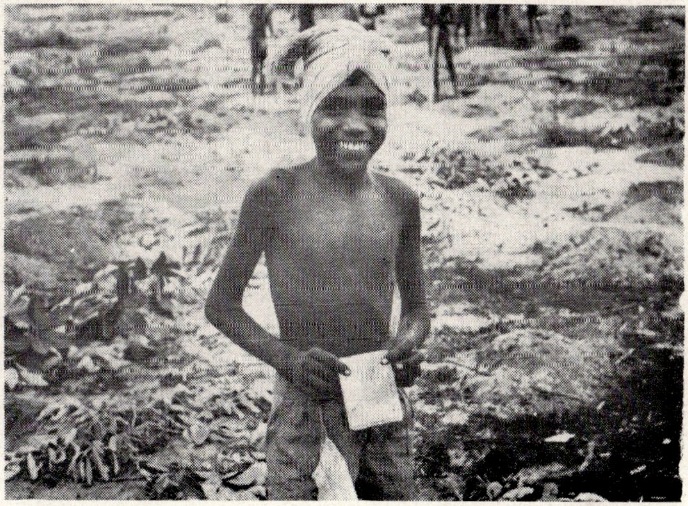

5. A Yanadi boy with a permanent pass *(See pages 48-49)*

6. Horticulture—an induced economy *(See pages 92-93)*

7. Yanadi women and non-Yanadi women engaged in horticulture *(See pages 84-86)*

6

Educational Support to Change

FOR GENERATIONS the Yanadi have been exploited by contractors, farmers, forest officials, and shopkeepers. To free them, the anthropologists searched for solutions in several directions. Imparting formal education in schools was considered important after having improvement in the means of survival. It was believed that economic development could hardly take place without education. The aim of education was to equip the Yanadi to fight against their exploitation, conceiving education to be a means and not an end in itself. As it was thought difficult to attract older Yanadi in the educational process, the approach of 'catch them young' was adopted. Not knowing how even the young children would respond to education, it was decided to study the reaction of Yanadi children and through them the Yanadi attitude towards education. This necessitated to establish an experimental school for Yanadi.

As discussed in Chapter 2, the British Government, and after Independence the state government, had made efforts to educate the Yanadi. In spite of a residential school, a few panchayat elementary schools, and a Thakkar Bapa Gurukulam sponsored by the Servants of India Society, very few Yanadi were educated up to fifth standard at the time of their rehabilitation.

Initial studies had given an indication that an experimental school could be tried out. In consultation with the Yanadi, the anthropologists in mid-1976 suggested that SHAR administration open a school. The SHAR Centre had neither funds nor was there provision for such a 'welfare activity'. However, SHAR administration was positively inclined to accept the proposal. Hence, the anthropologists initiated a dialogue with the Block Development Office, the agency responsible for primary education and rural schools. Though the Block Development Officer at Sullurpeta gladly accepted the proposal, yet he could not take any action as Sriharikota island was no more under the administrative control of the state government. Intervention of the Controller at Nellore, however, yielded results.

The anthropologists requested that the teacher of this sehool be a Yanadi because he could establish quick rapport with the children and other Yanadi. Initially the Block Development Officer could not find a qualified Yanadi teacher, though later he succeeded in selecting a matriculate Yanadi of Sullurpeta for this job. This person agreed to teach on a monthly salary of Rs. 260 and decided to commute everyday between SHAR and Sullurpeta.

Yanadi Experimental School (YES)

In the third week of July 1976, a Yanadi Experimental School started functioning at the B.N. Road habitation with the twin objectives of inculcating among the Yanadi the habit of sending children to school and also to initiate formal schooling for them. Further, it was thought that YES would provide an opportunity for Yanadi children to go to regular schools at a later stage. So it was decided to enroll all children regardless of age and sex. The B.N. Road habitation was chosen since it contained twentyfive Yanadi households who were working with a contractor. It was hoped that these Yanadi would continue to work with SHAR Centre even after the completion of the contract and would continue to stay at the same location.

To make the Yanadi feel at home, a thatched hut similar to a Yanadi hut was thought to be the most suitable structure. A hut, earlier used as cane depot by a contractor was cleaned for this purpose. A blackboard from the Space Central School, and a pair of cane chairs were all that the school was provided with. The Yanadi who showed willingness to send their children to school were consulted. But they expressed inability in buying writing slates, books and some clothes. The anthropologists assured them that the children would be provided with free slates, books, and clothes if they attended the school.

Twentyfour boys and girls were first enrolled whose ages ranged from five to twelve years. These children were provided with mid-day meals cooked by a Yanadi woman. It was thought that this would act as an incentive for the children to attend the school regularly. The total cost of the mid-day meal programme was borne by the Block Development Office. Contrary to hopes, the Yanadi of B.N. Road were not employed by SHAR administration for plantation work. So immediately on the completion of the contract work, the Yanadi started leaving B.N. Road habitation in search of work. This resulted in a gradual fall of the student enrollment. By December 1976, only thirteen students were on the rolls of the school. In order to increase the strength in the school, the anthropologists persuaded the Yanadi of Solladaruvu to shift to the B. N. Road location. This was accomplished in February 1977. The anthropologists visited every Yanadi household and explained the purpose of the school and requested them to send their children to the school. Soon the strength went up to thirtythree. In October 1977, the Yanadi of Maulam habitation also shifted to B.N. Road due to the death of a Yanadi. A few children of this newly migrated group also began to attend the school. This led to further increase in the strength from thirtythree to fortytwo.

During all these months, the anthropologists continued their efforts to emphasize the importance and advantages of education and talked to individuals whenever there was an opportunity. They demonstrated to the Yanadi as to how education was valuable for them in calculating wages, checking the accounts of the shopkeepers and purchasing provisions or repaying loans. It was also explained how the uneducated could easily be cheated. The anthropologists argued that if not the elders, at least the younger ones should be educated. After opening of the school, it was observed that the Yanadi children started spending most of their daytime in play at the school which was a natural extension of their habitation. Early morning, the children generally gathered at the school hut, eagerly waiting for the teacher. When the children saw the teacher coming at a distance some of them used to go and accompany him to the school. In the beginning, the adult Yanadi would gather near the school during the lunch break and enquire about the teacher's *intiperu* and his relatives. These elders were satisfied with the informal behaviour of the teacher with the children.

The children sat on the bare sands and learned Telugu which was closest to their language. Being a Yanadi, the teacher was aware of the consequences of beating and caning the children to discipline them. Therefore, he tried to teach the Yanadi children with an element of encouragement and mild intimidation of caning when the children committed repeated mistakes. The school hours came to a close at 4.30 in the afternoon. The irregularity on the part of the teacher led to a considerable fall in the attendance. If the teacher was absent for more than two consecutive days the attendance would fall below fifty per cent. On the first day, the children would gather at the school, and wait for the teacher till they realized that the usual arrival time of the teacher was over. Then they would start playing and going around the forest. As usual, the next day also they would gather at the school. If the teacher did not turn up on the second day also the children without gathering at the school would start playing on the third day.

It was observed that motivation for a child to go to school decreased as the distance between the hut and the school increased. This was due to the fact that children living near the school could not stay back in their huts as they were easily noticed by the teacher. Children living far away from the school could disappear from the sight of the teacher. Thus, the children living near the school were controlled by the teacher more than those who lived a little away. In order to provide continuity, on several occasions, the anthropologists themselves taught the children.

Knowing that a long break would affect the attendance, the anthropologists requested the Block Development Officer to permit the teacher to run the school even during the summer holidays. Though it was very unconventional, the Block Development Officer readily accepted this suggestion. The school was instituted on an *ad hoc* basis and in this way the unqualified teacher was able to draw salary for these months. Unfortunately, the Yanadi teacher resigned in November 1977.

As a result, the Yanadi Experimental School stopped functioning. Closure of the school within seventeen months of its inception was very disheartening. The Yanadi felt that their children would return to the original habits. The anthropologists felt that the school should be continued.

There were some gains and some failures in the running of the school. Even in this short period, it helped in attracting Yanadi children to school. This gave confidence to the anthropologists that they could bring about desirable changes among the Yanadi, provided proper direction was given. The most important lesson is that indigenization of an exogenous system into a community is necessary if it has to become an integral part of the environment in which the community lives. The closure of the school also weakened the new expectations of the Yanadi from the SHAR administration. The Yanadi had been expecting the closure of the school at any time. And when it came it gave support to their belief that the efforts to ameliorate Yanadi conditions were only an eyewash.

In spite of substantial efforts all the Yanadi children between 5 and 12 years of age could not attend the school. It was because the children of 10—12 years of age have to assist their parents in earning a living like those of contractors' work or to look after the younger ones while parents were working. Those children who stay back are asked to go for fishing or collecting forest food. Also parents did not insist upon or force the children to go to the school. The choice was left to the children themselves. So the dual factor like economic compulsion and individual choice of the child affected the total participation of the children in the school.

Voluntary school

The Yanadi Experimental School at B.N. Road habitation had a salutory effect on the Yanadi of Kalavagu habitation. They also wanted to have a school for their children and expressed this felt need to the anthropologists. The anthropologists suggested the institution of a voluntary school to be run and managed by the Yanadi themselves with a minimal of financial assistance. The anthropologists identified an educated Yanadi who was working in the Forestry and Horticulture Section as a casual labourer. He had studied in a Telugu medium school up to fifth grade. However, the anthropologists wanted to evaluate the readiness and interest of the Yanadi for the school. Therefore, they asked the Yanadi to erect a hut for the school. This was not necessary as the school was expected to run under the tree or in an open space. A large hut was erected within a couple of days. The school started functioning in January 1977. The anthropologists distributed writing slates to the children. One of the anthropologists stayed at Kalavagu for a couple of weeks and observed the functioning of the school. The teacher was regular and taught from 5.00 to 7.00 a.m. and 5.30 to 7.30 p.m. every day. In the morning, the children gathered near the hut of the teacher and sat in the open. He taught a few prayers which the children recited after him. When the teacher left for work, the children went to their huts. The children reassembled at the school hut on their own to read and write till noon. In the evening, the children would gather around a light fire and received their lessons in the alphabet. Thus the school hut was used only during the hot season and rains or when some officials visited the habitation.

In April 1977, a change in working hours made the teacher unavailable thereby leading to some disruption in the schedule. In July 1977, the school started functioning once again as the teacher was able to teach after work. The anthropologists made bi-weekly visits to the school. They examined the progress of each student and expressed their appreciation in the presence of the parents. They also asked the children to learn more before their next visit. This acted as encouragement to the children as well as to the parents. As the teacher was related to the students he was respected by all in the habitation. The teacher felt that a lamp and a few books would help to teach in the night. Before this need could be met by SHAR administration or the Yanadi Welfare Committee, the Yanadi themselves brought them. This clearly indicated the kind of interest the Yanadi took in education.

After the permanent rehabilitation in March 1978, the Yanadi of B.N. Road, Kalavagu and Penubakam were shifted to Penubakam. So the children of the voluntary and the experimental schools shifted to Penubakam where teaching in the voluntary school continued. But the children of the experimental school could not continue studies as the school had closed down. The anthropologists initiated the integration of these two schools and requested the voluntary school teacher to teach all the children of the habitation, including those who had not attended any school earlier. The strength of the school rose to fiftyone.

In the meantime, new problems arose. This included change in the workspot, the schedule of the teacher and large numbers of the students. Because of these new factors, the teacher could not devote much time towards the school for the next four months. At the same time, the anthropologists could not get the teacher off from the new work schedule even after repeated requests to SHAR administration as his services were considered essential. This necessitated an alternative arrangement for the school.

In order to cope with the situation and in continuation of the earlier efforts, the anthropologists met the Collector, Nellore once again along with SHAR officials and requested for the appointment of a teacher in August 1978. All these efforts went in vain when the new Collector took a negative decision and gave orders to abolish the Yanadi Experimental School. Lack of funds was given to be the reason for scrapping the school. However, this matter was kept under consideration at some future date in case of favourable financial situation. To solve this problem, a matriculate Yanadi and native of the island, was to be employed temporarily. The Yanadi Welfare Committee gladly accepted the suggestion of the anthropologists in this matter and decided to employ this Yanadi on a salary of Rs. 100 per month.

Yanadi experimental school (YES) born again

With the appointment of a new teacher, the Yanadi Experimental School was restarted under a tree at Penubakam in August 1978. Now the teacher was staying at Penubakam. Midday meal was also restarted in January 1979 with the persistent efforts of the Yanadi Welfare Committee. On October 9, 1978, the Yanadi Experimental School was shifted to a permanent multipurpose building. In the beginning, the teacher took keen interest but gradually his interest faded away. At the same time, there were problems of having an unmarried Yanadi as a teacher who was staying in the same habitation. One of the major problems was that he got involved in petty quarrels with other Yanadi, as he wanted to marry a girl who had been studying in the school. His involvement with the girl created embarrassment to the other children and elders. He could no more command respect as a teacher and gradually his image as a teacher was tarnished.

During the year, the Yanadi teacher started working for SHAR Centre as an attendant from May 1980. The Yanadi Welfare Committee met in May 1980 and discussed the possibility of appointing another teacher. The anthropologists favoured the appointment of a retired teacher on the grounds of effectiveness. But one of the members suggested a non-Yanadi who was like a Yanadi in many ways, and educated up to matriculation. He was a casual labourer and had come to the island about eight years ago in search of a job. Though doubts about the suitability of this person were expressed by the anthropologists, the Yanadi Welfare Committee decided to take him from June 1, 1980. Later, the anthropologists found that the non-Yanadi teacher was a good choice. This new teacher has had remarkable influence on the school, the students and the Yanadi. His skill as a farmer and understanding of the Yanadi, combined with maturity gave him a very special place among the Yanadi. The Yanadi were impressed with the teacher's behaviour and hard work and they could not talk but highly of him. Though the teacher stayed in Kothachenu, he ran the school regularly and punctually everyday. He was quick to establish rapport with the students and their parents. He was able to introduce cleanliness among the students by introducing the mid-day bath. The Yanadi believe that taking cold water bath in the morning leads to sickness. Therefore, instructions to come to school after taking bath were ignored by the Yanadi children. But once the mid-day bath concept was introduced the children were found taking bath regularly from the hand pump behind the school building during lunch break. Every morning he checked the presence of every child and those who did not come to school were personally brought by him excepting the ones who were sick.

He also grew a kitchen garden on the advice of the

anthropologists. This became a symbol of collective effort of the children and the teacher. At the same time, it provided fruits and vegetables for the mid-day meals. Though Yanadi children are very individualistic, they worked collectively on the kitchen garden. From clearing the jungle, tilling the land, manuring, sowing and watering the plants to harvesting everything was done by the students. It was impressive to see a very green patch of land by the side of school after two months. It was almost a demonstration plot for the Yanadi and a learning ground for the children. At the same time, it provided means of constructively channelizing the energy of the children. The support of the Forestry and Horticulture Section was important as they provided seeds, though after repeated requests. It seems that continuity of activities provides the essence of learning among the Yanadi. It is for this reason that a variety of activities which included learning in school, doing horticulture work, home work, and taking bath were positively accepted by the Yanadi children. The kitchen garden became the expression of their collective efforts whereas the school was the place for learning and other activities. It was no accident that the children studied in the school without supervision.

YES teaching method

For teaching the alphabet, the teacher writes two letters on the slate and then the student is asked to identify them. He holds the hand of the child and writes over what he has written, telling him or her how to hold the pencil, where to make a loop where to start and end the letter, and how to hold the slate. The teacher supervises how the child starts writing the letters and whether the slate is kept correctly. If he finds any mistake, he corrects the child. After writing several times, the child is asked to write separately and then on the back of the slate without looking at the letter. When the child writes well and tells the name of the letter, the teacher goes on to the next letters.

Lessons

After learning the alphabet, the students starts writing and reading simple words. The teacher gathers all the students who have completed learning of the alphabet and reads slowly each word. The students repeat the word. He corrects their pronunciation and explains if the word is not in their daily use. He also tells how to write combinations of different sounds and words. Then the students go to their respective places and copy the words from the textbook. While doing so, they read aloud.

Dictation

After the students have learnt to identify letters and write words the teacher starts dictating words from the textbook. The students are expected to write them without referring to the text-book. All of them have to close their books and be ready to write what the teacher asks them to write. The teacher spells out a word, repeats it and gives time for the students to recapitulate the letters and the word. After dictating ten or fifteen words the teacher asks the students to pile up their slates. He then corrects the wrong words.

Arithmetic

For teaching arithmetic, the teacher writes five numerals on the slate and tells their names. The students learn the numerals. When the child is able to write from 1 to 1000 he is taught simple calculations of addition and subtraction. First the additions start with single rows of digits. The student is asked to put marks as 'one' against each set of digits. After putting the marks to all sets of digits, the marks are counted. When the students get familiar with this method, the teacher asks them not to put marks but to count on the fingers, corresponding to each set of digits. After learning the additions of single rows of numerals, the two number set rows and then three number set rows and the like are taught by a similar method. In the same way, subtraction is taught. First the deductions start with the help of marks and later with fingers. When the students have learnt addition and subtraction, they are taught multiplication tables. In this case, the teacher writes the table on the slate. As the students identify each number, they read the table fluently. By repeated reading and memorising, the students learn the table by heart. As the child learns the first table, the next higher table is taught. Thus each student learns the tables from two to twenty. By way of dictation and also by writing daily the teacher helps them to keep them in memory. After learning multiplication tables large multiplication and division sums are taught.

Pronouncing and repetition method

This is a very effective method of teaching. It is followed in two ways. One is with the help of blackboard and the other is without the blackboard. All the alphabets, names of the days, months are written on the board by the teacher. One of the boys who had learnt them already, points out the alphabets and the words and pronounces loudly. This is repeated by the rest of the students. This is practised every evening. The blackboard is not used for multiplication tables as they require a lot of space. So in this case the children who know the tables, repeat them while the rest of the students repeat irrespective of their learning stage. In this method of recitation, names of days, months, nursery rhymes both in Telugu and English are taught.

Homework

Every day before coming to school in the morning, the children who are learning the alphabet should write them on their slates and come to school. If the child has learnt the alphabet the individual writes whatever is being learnt, be it a lesson, numerical numbers or multiplication tables. The teacher advises the children to study or write in the morning as soon as they get up from sleep. During lunch break, the students who are learning or who have learnt should write the multiplication tables without referring to the book before the evening session of the school starts. The teacher corrects homework of all the students, before starting teaching in the ensuing session.

Extra-curricular activities

The teacher gets the floor of the school building washed at least once a week. The girls have to sweep the room every day. The surroundings of the school building are kept clean by the students as directed by the teacher. An area of half an acre has been cleared of the bushes for the playground. The teacher advises the students often that if they study well they will get good jobs, and go to hospital for all the ailments. He tells them to take bath daily and comb their hair. The student who comes to school without combing his hair is sent back home for combing it. The school sports include *khc-kho*, imitation game, musical chairs and drill in addition to the traditional Yanadi games. Throughout the teaching, the teacher talks and instructs the students without hurting their feelings and caning. When he gets angry, in the beginning he intimidated them to beat but he never did. Later having acquired the confidence and respect from the students he did slap them once in a while but the students never took it seriously and the teacher also immediately cajoled them. On the advice of the anthropologists the teacher allowed the children wherever they wanted to go out for urination or for drinking water. This facilitated them to be free from long time sitting and strain.

State take over of the YES

The state government sanctioned a teacher's post for the Yanadi Experimental School in October 1980 and posted the same teacher who had earlier taught at the Panchayat Elementary School at Pitcharigunta and Kothachenu. The anthropologists were alerted about this appointment as this teacher was found to be dishonest and not sincere in his work, and was frequently absenting himself from work while at Kothachenu. He had not been sympathetic towards the Yanadi children. He had also mismanaged the stocks of the Special Nutrition Programme at Kothachenu. Knowing these problems, the Yanadi Welfare Committee decided to continue the non-Yanadi teacher as an assistant teacher. In order to minimize conflicts, the non-Yanadi teacher was asked to maintain the kitchen garden and teach one of the classes. In addition, he was asked to help the Yanadi in formalities connected with bank loan return and other accounts. Let us see how this new experiment worked.

Panchayat elementary school

Pitcharigunta habitation had both Yanadi and non-Yanadi. The non-Yanadi exceeded numerically over the Yanadi. There was already a private school run by a non-Yanadi resident who charged a fee of Rs. 3 per child per month. There were fifteen non-Yanadi children in the school. The Yanadi could not send their children to the private school. However, they strongly expressed their desire to get their children educated. The anthropologists requested Assistant Administrative Officer (Welfare) to open another school at Pitcharigunta, which started functioning in July 1977 exactly one year after the Yanadi Experimental School was started. In this school, fifteen Yanadi and thirty-five non-Yanadi children were admitted. It was like any other school run by the state government with strict adherence to timings and syllabus. The Yanadi believe that the cane is a weapon that gods use to beat devils with. Therefore, the non-Yanadi teacher was requested to avoid the use of cane on the Yanadi children. The parents were also given assurances that their children would be spared from the cane.

The school hut was located at a distance of 200 metres from the Yanadi huts. The school was provided with a table, a chair and a clock. The teacher also lived in the same habitation. The school started at 7.30 a.m and the children were expected to be in the school latest by 7.45 a.m. The morning session lasted from 7.45 to 11.00 a.m. with a ten minute interval. The evening session lasted from 2.30 to 4.30 p.m. again with a ten minute interval at 3.50 p.m. In the initial stages, the Yanadi children found it uncomfortable at long sittings. They quite often went out on the pretext of going to the toilet. The teacher also punished the errant non-Yanadi students physically. This scared away the Yanadi children. All this led to a constant fear among the Yanadi children of the teacher.

The non-Yanadi children were quite expressive in the class. They always came forward to initiate the recital of the alphabets. The Yanadi children felt inferior in their presence and would not respond to the teacher unless they were called for. The Yanadi children would not also answer questions fearing flogging if they made a mistake. Owing to the fear, the Yanadi children would not submit their slates for correction. In addition, the teacher did not take proper care of the Yanadi children. So the teacher was finding it difficult to teach the Yanadi children. It was observed that he was not kind and sympathetic to the Yanadi children.

When the Panchayat Elementary School came into existence, the private school ceased to function. The children of the private school joined the Panchayat Elementary School due to which it became crowded having four classes with one teacher.

Hence, the teacher, was unable to devote sufficient time to teach the Yanadi children. As there was only one blackboard, reading by one child and its repetition by the rest was not possible. After the permanent settlement, the Panchayat Elementary School was shifted to Kothachenu and started functioning in an old forest guest-house from March 1978. This building is nearly fifty metres away from the Yanadi habitation towards the east. After the shifting, the problems of the Yanadi children were accentuated owing to the enormous increase in the school strength mostly non-Yanadi, Most of the Yanadi children were detained in class one, even after the completion of the first academic year. This was done because the teacher felt that the Yanadi children were not regular in class, did not show interest, and also showed less concentration in studies. To solve some of these problems, the anthropologists suggested that the classes one and two which consisted of the Yanadi children should meet in the morning from 7.30 a.m. to 11.00 a.m. and classes three and four from 2 to 4.30 p.m. This suggestion was turned down by the Block Development Officer as it was regarded as unconventional. So to overcome this problem, the anthropologists started teaching the Yanadi children in the morning and evening from March 1978 to April 1979. This approach helped the situation to some extent but was not very satisfactory.

Telugu medium primary school

As a result of the combined efforts of the SHAR centre employees and the SHAR administration, the state government sanctioned a Telugu medium primary school for SHAR. The Panchayat Samiti Elementary School functioning at Kothachenu was merged with this school in April 1979.

A new school building was constructed half a kilometre away from Kothachenu towards SHAR employees housing colony known as Temporary Housing Colony. This school had five classes and the strength of the school rose to more than 250 students by the end of 1979. The children of Kothachenu had to walk half a kilometre to attend the school both in the morning and in the evening. The anthropologists were unhappy over this development because, as indicated earlier, distance was identified to be one of the most important deterring factors for the Yanadi children. The Yanadi children became irregular in the school. They often complained that the non-Yanadi children beat them. As the school was away from the habitation, the control of the teacher over the children was completely lost. It was observed that the Yanadi felt completely lost in the midst of overcrowded non-Yanadi classrooms. The impersonal and formal relations of the teachers also made them irregular in the school, though the teacher made efforts to make these children regular in the class.

Results

Inadequate finance and lack of appreciation on the part of the state government led to various disruptions and discontinuity in the total educational effort. Vague policies of the SHAR administration, though sympathetic, disrupted the voluntary efforts to run the school. In spite of certain difficulties, the cumulative effect of the total effort of four years, though very meagre yielded some positive results in the education of the Yanadi children.

Table 6.1 shows the year-wise strength of the total Yanadi children in various schools between 1976 to 1980.

TABLE 6.1 : STRENGTH OF YANADI CHILDREN IN SCHOOLS

Number of Each Year	Yanadi Experimental School			Voluntary School			Panchayat Elementary/ Telugu Medium School			Total		
	B	G	T	B	G	T	B	G	T	B	G	T
1976	7	6	13	—	—	—	—	—	—	7	6	13
1977	27	15	42	14	11	25	7	8	15	48	34	82
1978	29	22	51	—	—	—	6	6	12	35	28	63
1979	20	13	33	—	—	—	9	6	15	29	19	48
1980	24	14	38	—	—	—	9	4	13	33	18	51

B—Boys. G—Girls. T—Total.

There were fluctuations in the student strength. The maximum number of children went to school in 1977. The main reasons for decrease of school strength after 1977 were

(i) thirteen grown-up children left the school to help their parents in earning, (ii) two children were admitted to Sishuvihar, and (iii) nearly fifteen children stopped attending the school when their parents left the habitation. Out of 112 children in the school-going age, 82 children went to school, which is a little over 73 per cent.

An effort was also made to analyse various levels of educational achievements by the Yanadi children in these four years. In 1978, when the first attempt was made to analyse their educational achievements, it was observed that the older children were able to learn faster than the younger ones leading to differential educational achievements in the same class. In order to analyse this differential learning, the Yanadi children were asked to read and write various textbooks of Class I, Class II, Class III and Class IV, prescribed by the state government for Telugu medium schools.

TABLE 6.2 : YANADI CHILDREN IN DIFFERENT STAGES OF LEARNING

Stages of Learning	1978-79			1979-80			1980-81		
	B	G	T	B	G	T	B	G	T
Learning of Telugu alphabet-only	14	19	33	8	7	15	9	5	14
Reading of Telugu Class I book and learning of numbers	19	4	23	13	6	19	13	11	24
Reading of Telugu Class II and learning of simple arithmetic	3	4	7	6	4	10	3	1	4
Studying Class III books	—	—	—	2	2	4	6	—	6
Studying Class IV books	—	—	—	—	—	—	2	1	3
Total	36	27	63	29	19	48	33	18	51

B—Boys. G—Girls. T—Total.

According to the table during 1980, 14 students were learning Telugu alphabets and 25 were able to read Class I Telugu textbooks and count and write numbers. Three children were able to read Telugu Class II textbooks and knew simple addition and subtraction. Six children were

8. Water for horticulture *(See pages 84-86)*

9. Poultry farming—a new source of income *(See pages 90-91)*

10. Yanadi women at the handpump *(See pages 52-53)*

11. Sudhakar Rao joining the Yanadi *malam* group *(See pages 6-8)*

studying Class III Telugu general science, social studies and mathematics books. The Table 6.2 further indicates that some of the children who had joined the Yanadi Experimental School and other schools in 1976 and 1977 had progressed well in the last three years and had achieved educational levels similar to those of the non-Yanadi. The table records a gradual fall in the number of students in Stage I for the last three years. The table makes it also clear that the progress of the girl students was poor and even their strength had gradually reduced. The main reason was that the girls when they become older stopped attending the school and remained at home. They felt that they were old enough to look after household affairs.

It may be interesting to note that songs and prayers taught to these children were in Sanskrit. The *slokas* were recited in honour of Lord Vishnu. Another song was the national anthem in Hindi. The third song was about the praise of the State of Andhra Pradesh, its people, land, and language. The content analysis of these prayers and songs shows that whatever the Yanadi children learnt was alien in language and tradition. What the implications of such learning are we do not know at this stage. But one can argue that this would facilitate gradual assimilation and integration of the Yanadi in Hindu society.

In the initial stages, the parents and the children were casual about school attendance. Gradually, a growing interest among the parents was observed. During this period, the importance of education was explained to them by the anthropologists. The Yanadi also learned that educated co-workers got regular employment in SHAR Centre. The Yanadi began to take interest in the school and showed concern whenever the teacher failed to come to school. The presence of school also brought changes in the lifestyle of the Yanadi children. The teachers instructed the children to clean their faces and comb their hair before coming to school. Thus, the children learnt a bit of cleanliness even though most of them were unclean and had scanty clothes. It is obvious that the compulsory attendance in the school weaned the children from going to the forests. This may lead to the loss of the children's ability to recognize plants and herbs. Further to less participation in the exploitation of the forest food and thereby loss of capabilities of its exploitation.

Scholarships

The Andhra Pradesh Government provides scholarships to school-going tribal children through the district tribal reclamation officer. It was thought that scholarships would encourage the Yanadi children to attend the school. Therefore, the anthropologists with the help of the Yanadi Welfare Committee tried to procure scholarships for Yanadi children. The application forms were collected from the Block Development Officer, Sullurpeta. As the Yanadi Experimental School teacher had resigned by that time, the applications were sent through the Panchayat Elementary School, Pitcharigunta, though it was unconventional. Because of the goodwill of tribal reclamation officer, all the school-going Yanadi children were sanctioned scholarships.

The applications for scholarships had to be accompanied with caste and income certificates. As the island is no more under the revenue jurisdiction of the state, the Tahsildar of Sullurpeta Taluka was not willing to sign the caste and income certificates. After discussion with the Tahsildar and the SHAR administration, it was agreed that income certificates would be given by the head of the Forestry and Horticulture Section and caste certificates by the convener of the Yanadi Welfare Committee. These two certificates would be countersigned

TABLE 6.3 : YEARWISE SCHOLARSHIP-HOLDERS BY CLASS

Year	Total Number of students	Scholarships Awarded		
		Class I	Class II and above	Total
1976-77	13	—	—	—
1977-78	57*	42	—	42
1978-79	68	15	33	48
1979-80	48	15	—	15
1980-81	51	4	9	13

*Students of voluntary school are excluded.

by the Senior Administrative Officer, and finally by the Tahsildar. Thus, the applications had to pass through different officials before reaching the Tribal Reclamation officer.

Table 6.3 shows that, in each year, not all students were awarded scholarships. Though the state government had sanctioned scholarships for all, the anthropologists restricted them to those who were regular throughout the year. This was done to encourage regular school attendance. It can also be observed from the table that in 1979-80 and 1980-81 only fifteen and thirteen students respectively were given scholarships. In those years students attending the Telugu Medium School run by the Panchayat Samiti alone were given scholarships. Though the state government had renewed scholarships to all Yanadi students, the Deputy Inspector of Schools raised objection against the students attending the Yanadi Experimental School on the ground that the school was not run by the state government. Fresh applications for scholarships from Yanadi Experimental School students were rejected by the new Reclamation Officer for the same reason. When the Yanadi Experimental School was taken over by the state government in October 1980, fresh attempts were made to sanction scholarships to students of the Yanadi Experimental School for 1979-80 and 1980-81. Though the scholarships encouraged the parents to send their children to school, it failed to attract fresh students to the school.

The above analysis regarding the attempts made to impart formal education to the Yanadi clearly shows various administrative problems and cultural constraints in implementing the anthropologists' suggestions. The results indicate significant gains in educating the Yanadi. It has been proved beyond doubt that Yanadi children are no less equal to any other in learning process, provided a congenial atmosphere is created for them. The school was found to be a 'golden threshold' to use a Yanadi metaphor, to equip themselves to adapt to the non-Yanadi world.

7

Transformation of Yanadi Economy

THE ANALYSIS presented in Chapter 4 indicates that the Yanadi suffered from immense economic backwardness virtually bordering on squalor. A lot of efforts had to be put in to ameliorate this economic distress and ways and means had to be devised to remove their poverty. A two pronged strategy of employment to all able-bodied Yanadi round the year on daily wage rates prescribed by the government and development of sources of additional income to minimize total dependence on daily wage employment.

Employment

Daily wage work

Daily wage employment in SHAR Centre is provided by the Forestry and Horticulture Section, Public Health Section and Canteen Section. The Forestry and Horticulture Section looks after maintenance and raising of plantations in forest; collection of forest produce; clearing of jungle and beautification works like development of gardens and lawns. The area of operations being very vast, a large number of labourers are required for these works. The Public Health Section requires labour for garbage disposal, spraying of anti-mosquito chemicals and DDT, and sweeping housing colonies and office premises. In the Canteen Section, labour is required for cleaning and dishwashing. Year round labour is required for all these works. In spite of all these employment avenues, out of 294 able-bodied persons, only 140 Yanadi were working with SHAR administration in the fall of 1975. On an average, one able-bodied person was employed from each household.

Numerically, more non-Yanadi than the Yanadi were employed even for these works. It was observed that the Yanadi would not approach the officials of the Forestry and Horticulture Section for jobs. On the contrary, the non-Yanadi would approach and persuade them to provide jobs. At the same time, the preconceived notions of the forest officials about the Yanadi as indicated in Chapter 4 became an important hindrance in providing them jobs.

In order to provide full employment to the Yanadi, it became imperative for us to locate possible jobs on the island which suited the Yanadi and which they could perform with proficiency. Time and again, SHAR Centre officials had indicated that the Yanadi were most suited for forest-related works as in their opinion the "Yanadi knew the forest most intimately and liked to work in the forest". In order to secure jobs for the Yanadi in the forest it was essential that the Yanadi must be given preference over the non-Yanadi during lean employment periods and that all forest activities must be done by SHAR administration through its Forestry and Horticulture Section. The anthropologists tried to convince the forest officials to hire the Yanadi during lean employment periods and at the same time convinced Chairman, ISRO to take a policy decision on hiring Yanadi for forest-related work. The Chairman also decided that "there will be no laying off of the Yanadi from jobs, instead they will be given alternate jobs". In order to implement this decision, the anthropologists remained continuously in touch with the Forestry and Horticulture Section, and tried to get employment for the Yanadi as and when and wherever possible. In this role, the anthropologists acted as a link between the Yanadi and SHAR administration.

In the process, the anthropologists were accused of recommending those Yanadi who had been irregular in the discharge of their duties. So the anthropologists had to plead with them time and again to be regular. Another difficulty was that the Yanadi labourers who absented from work for few weeks due to sickness were not re-employed quickly. The same was true of pregnant and lactating mothers. The anthropologists had to approach the forest officials and convince them to re-employ such Yanadi without much delay. The forest officials now and then diverted the forest labour from one workspot to another, according to their requirements. This resulted in several kilometres of walk for the Yanadi. The anthropologists were successful in re-arranging the workspots.

There were some Yanadi labourers who were treated as boy *majdoors* (labourers) and were paid lower wages. To be treated as an adult of more than 18 years of age, they required age certificate from the revenue officials. As the island is no more under state control, the revenue officials could not provide this certificate. To overcome this problem, the anthropologists consulted SHAR hospital doctors who after medical examination, gave the required age certificate. This helped two boy *majdoors* to earn wages of adult labourers. In 1976, the daily wages for female labourers were one rupee less than that of male labourers. The anthropologists demanded that females should be paid same wages as that of male labourers in accordance with government rules. This demand was accepted by SHAR administration and equal wages were paid from June 1978 on.

The efforts of the anthropologists in soliciting cooperation from the Forestry and Horticulture Section resulted in providing somewhat regular employment to many Yanadi. The Forestry and Horticulture Section also accepted the suggestion to start collection of forest produce by employing Yanadi daily wage labourers from 1977 onwards. It helped in removing the middle-men contractors who were exploiting the Yanadi.

TABLE 7.1 : YEAR-WISE EMPLOYMENT OF LABOURERS IN SHAR CENTRE

	Total number of persons employed in a year					
Category	1975	1976	1977	1978	1979	1980
Yanadi	140	215	275	252	129	64
Non-Yanadi	247	226	237	246	176	147

The number of Yanadi employed showed an increase from 1975 to 1977 and started reducing in 1978 and steeply in 1980. It was maximum in 1977 because the Forestry and Horticulture

Section had accepted the anthropologists' suggestion of collecting forest produce by employing Yanadi labourers. However, after the completion of forest produce collection, the surplus labour were gradually relieved. The anthropologists put the problem before the Yanadi Welfare Committee with the suggestion that only non-Yanadi labourers belonging to the households of regular employees should be relieved if it was essential and this request was readily conceded.

In spite of this measure, Yanadi labour strength decreased from 275 in 1977 to 252 in 1978. It was because the contract for the collection of forest produce was partly given to the contractors in that year who had hired other Yanadi. In 1979 and 1980, there was a steep fall in labour strength in general, including the Yanadi. During these years, plantation work was contracted out to the contractors. The Yanadi preferred to work with them and left the Forestry and Horticulture Section.

Public health employment

In 1976, nearly thirty-two Yanadi were sent from the Forestry and Horticulture Section to work in the Public Health Section. They slowly stopped going to work one after another. Investigations revealed that the Yanadi did not enjoy working on garbage disposal. On the contrary, they loathed the very smell of garbage. It was also observed that most of them fell sick quite often while working on garbage disposal. The Yanadi began to despise garbage work and also were found irregular either due to sickness or because of the dislike for the job. In spite of higher daily wages in the Public Health Section, the Yanadi preferred to work in the Forestry and Horticulture Section, as they were accustomed to forest work. Given an opportunity, they preferred to work with the contractors since there was no control on regularity and timings.

Higher daily wages

From the very beginning it was thought that increase of wages would help the Yanadi in improving the means of survival. The anthropologists took up this matter with the forest officials and with SHAR administration. The daily wages paid until December 1976, to an adult male labour working in the Public Health and Canteen Sections were Rs. 5 per day whereas an adult male labour working in the Forestry and Horticulture Section was paid Rs. 4. An adult female labour, in Forestry and Horticulture Section received Rs. 3 whereas the boys and girls received Rs. 2.50 per day. Due to the pressure exerted by the anthropologists, the wages were raised in December 1976. Accordingly, adult female labourer was paid Rs. 4 and the boys or girls were paid Rs. 3. After two weeks, wages for adult male labourers were further raised to Rs. 4.25 and Rs. 3 for girls. In the meanwhile, the SHAR administration began consulting the state government about the minimum wages.

As no changes in the wage structure was forthcoming, the non-Yanadi labourers went on strike for a day in the fall of 1979. They were supported by the SHAR Employees Union. Because of this mounting pressure, the daily wages were raised once again from Rs. 4.25 to Rs. 4.45 and the concept of equal wages for both sexes was implemented in June 1979. Again in October 1980, the wages were raised to Rs. 5.10 for both sexes in the Forestry and Horticulture Section and Rs. 5.75 for labourers in the Public Health and Canteen Sections.

Regular employment

Several administrative problems were faced in securing regular jobs for the Yanadi in SHAR Centre. All recruitment in Indian Space Research Organization for the posts below a basic salary of Rs. 425 per month is made through the District Employment Exchange. The same procedure is followed in SHAR Centre for recruitment to the posts of gardeners, sweepers, attendants, clerks, and certain categories of technical staff. None of the Yanadi in 1976 was registered in the Employment Exchange, except three. Further, most of them could not fulfil the educational requirement of eighth standard, though a number of young Yanadi were competent gardeners. In order to get regular employment, the Yanadi had to register their names in the District Employment Exchange, Nellore, which is about 120 kilometres from SHAR. For going to Nellore, each Yanadi had to spend Rs. 15 leaving aside the difficulties ... completing the formalities of getting registered. In spite of these difficulties, three Yanadi were able to register their names. To overcome this problem, the Employment Officer, Nellore, was requested to visit SHAR Centre for registering the Yanadi through the Yanadi Welfare Committee. The Employment Officer visited SHAR Centre in May 1978 and registered the names of the majority of the Yanadi by visiting their habitations.

Since many of the Yanadi are illiterate, the anthropologists requested SHAR administration to waive educational requirements for the post of sweepers and gardeners. The Yanadi Welfare Committee also supported this idea. As expected, this request was turned down by SHAR administration. In the next three years, even the educated Yanadi were not called for regular jobs whereas some of the non-Yanadi were called. This was because the non-Yanadi had registered their names much earlier. The Yanadi were unhappy when they were not called for interview. It was left to the anthropologists to convince the Yanadi to wait for their chance to come.

The exception was a Yanadi working as casual labourer in the canteen. He was called for interview for the post of 'canteen boy' in the fall of 1977. He was educated up to standard seven. Relaxation made in the educational qualifications at the highest level helped his appointment in early 1978. It took more than six months after he was initially interviewed to obtain relaxation in educational qualifications. It may be pointed out that these regulations are such that they require a very strong administrative support for making any exception. In May 1980, seven Yanadi were sponsored by the District Employment Exchange for an interview for the post of *safaiwala* (sweepers) in SHAR Centre. All of them were selected but only four of them were offered daily wage work at the rate of Rs. 5 per day and that too for about a month during June-July, 1980. Even this would not have taken place had not the anthropologists been actively involved and the Yanadi Welfare Committee members taken special interest.

In April 1980, when the anthropologists came to know about the appointment of a score of sweepers in SHAR Centre, they with the support of the Yanadi Welfare Committee went to Nellore to find out whether the Yanadi in District Employment Exchange were sponsored and if not, request the officer to do so. On the first visit the officer was out of town. On the second visit the anthropologists found that none of the Yanadi were sponsored as they did not fulfil the minimum educational qualifications up to the standard. Also the list of sponsored candidates had already been sent to SHAR administration. The anthropologists were surprised to hear this as there were few Yanadi who had education up to standard five. When this was pointed out to the Employment Officer, he replied that they might not have renewed their registration. Also they might not have indicated their educational qualifications at the time of registration. The anthropologists returned in dismay only to find that the Yanadi had been renewing their registration. The Yanadi were also surprised to hear the news. Though the Yanadi had no money, they had to go to Nellore again. The next day they went to the District Employment Exchange accompanied by one of the anthropologists. A member of the Yanadi Welfare Committee and the other anthropologists met officials of SHAR administration and explained the difficulties of the Yanadi registered with the Employment Exchange. They requested to accept a second list of sponsored candidates from the Employment Exchange.

The Employment Officer was able to find the missing registration and renewal papers of the Yanadi and was sorry to have misplaced them. A few days later he sponsored the names of seven Yanadi for the post of *safaiwala* (sweeper). The Yanadi were intimated individually about the interview. But they had to face another difficulty of obtaining caste and nativity certificates. The Yanadi went to the Taluka Office, Sullurpeta and requested their old village *munsif* to issue them the certificates. The Yanadi had to visit Sullurpeta thrice because the concerned officials were absent. Three Yanadi were asked to give Rs. 25 each as a 'favour' for issuing the certificates. Also all the Yanadi were required to produce three passport size photographs which cost Rs. 10 each. For two of them the anthropologists lent the money.

The interview was held on May 29, 1980. All the seven Yanadi were selected but after a couple of weeks, four Yanadi were offered daily wage work for a month. When the services of the four Yanadi were terminated, the anthropologists and members of the Yanadi Welfare Committee met the Controller and requested him to provide them with regular jobs. He replied that these seven Yanadi would remain in a panel for one year and whenever there was a regular vacancy it would be filled by them.

The analyses indicate how cumbersome, time consuming and money-consuming is the procedure of employment. Even though Yanadi who have had the support of the anthropologists and the Yanadi Welfare Committee they had great difficulty in getting a job.

Sources of additional income

Poultry and goat rearing

Early analysis in Chapter 4 has indicated that raising poultry and goats, which required very little supervision and capital, could be additional sources of income. Eggs and poultry were expected to supplement the diet and also could be sold to the non-Yanadi as there was a demand for them in the island. It was observed that the island was an ideal place for raising goats. Also there was a good market for goats in and outside the island. Due to lack of financial resources, the Yanadi could not do poultry farming and particularly goats and there was nobodyto encourage them. Initially, the anthropologists encouraged the Yanadi to raise poultry and goats. They explained to the Yanadi as to how raising of these would add to their household income.

In 1977 a goat was given by the anthropologists to an interested Yanadi. After twenty months he could return the money by selling the offspring of the goat. In April 1978, another goat was gifted to a Yanadi girl for her domestic services. The anthropologists purchased four hens and gave them for raising to another Yanadi who later returned the cost of the hens. Because of the financial constraints in taking up this programme, the anthropologists felt that the Yanadi should be given loans from the nationalized banks. However, this could not be arranged owing to a large number of technical and operational difficulties.

In December 1976, five Yanadi households were raising

poultry and six households were raising goats on their own. Table 7.2 shows the households raising poultry and goats in the last five years as a result of efforts made by the anthropologists.

TABLE 7.2 : HOUSEHOLD RAISING OF POULTRY AND GOATS

Month of data Collection	Number of households	Number of birds	Number of households	Number of goats
December 1976	5	20	6	18
November 1977	25	50	9	35
April 1978	79	291	14	119
June 1978	65	177	15	120
July 1979	55	190	17	132
July 1980	63	187	21	118

Most of the Yanadi borrowed a hen or goat from another Yanadi household or a non-Yanadi for rearing. The offspring were shared equally between the caretaker and the owner. This method of borrowing did not involve any initial investment. A few Yanadi households also purchased one or two hens and multiplied them by rearing. Table 7.2 shows that the number of households raising poultry is more than the ones raising goats. It is so because goat rearing requires higher investments which the Yanadi at present are not in a position to afford. Domestic poultry raising started mostly by borrowing chickens from the other households as indicated earlier.

During April and May 1978, the hens were affected by a disease and 114 of these died. The number of households raising poultry was reduced to 65 in June 1978. The death of the birds discouraged some of the Yanadi households to raise them and that is why there was no increase in 1979 and 1980. It is also because of the menace of jackals which led to the loss of 39 hens in 1980. Table 7.3 shows the number of households which sold poultry produce and income received between 1977 and 1980.

Table 7.4 shows the frequency of households which sold goats and their income and expenditure. It may be observed that large expenditure was made on provisions and clothes. Some money was also spent on ornaments.

TABLE 7.3 : YEARLY INCOME THROUGH REARING POULTRY

Year	Number of households	Income (Rs)
1977	2	28
1978	5	141
1979	16	500
1980	11	365

Through experience the Yanadi realised that poultry and goats would help them in dark days. It was observed that whenever a person fell sick or was unable to work for a week or two, he sold his poultry and goats to buy provisions. For those who worked regularly, income from poultry and goats came in handy buying more clothes and household possessions like utensils and knives. The Yanadi to some extent eat eggs and poultry also. This has helped increase the quantity and quality of food intake which would improve their health standards after some time. The SHAR employees are drawn to Yanadi habitations for buying poultry and goats. This has led to higher interaction between SHAR employees and the Yanadi.

TABLE 7.4 : EXPENDITURE ON AND INCOME FROM GOAT REARING

Year	No. of households	No. of goats sold	Income (Rs.)	Expenditure: Debt paid (Rs.)	Provisions (Rs.)	Clothes (Rs.)	Medicine (Rs.)	Lending (Rs.)	Miscellaneous (Rs.)
1977	1	2	250	100	100	50	—	—	—
1978	4	7	1,000	370	190	175	30	145	90
1979	3	10	1,300	—	620	180	200	—	300
1980	10	17	2,405	—	870	370	200	100	310

Horticulture

Agriculture was thought to be another important means of additional income. Knowing that agriculture was prohibited by SHAR administration and that the Yanadi lacked experience, horticulture was suggested as an alternative. It was also thought that horticulture would be less capital intensive as compared to agriculture. In December 1976, it was observed that six Yanadi had grown vegetables near their huts. This showed that the Yanadi had aptitude and desire for growing vegetables and other plants. The anthropologists thought of encouraging the Yanadi to grow various kinds of vegetables to supplement their diet.

Effort

To initiate action, anthropologists wanted to provide free seeds to the Yanadi. They requested the Head of the Forestry and Horticulture Section to spare some vegetable seeds. Small quantities of seeds of chillies, leafy vegetables, tomatoes, bottle gourds, snake gourds, ridged gourds, and pumpkins were provided by them. Instead of issuing seeds to every Yanadi household, the anthropologists informed them that whosoever was interested could collect the necessary quantity of seeds. This was done so as to indicate to the Yanadi that they should not consider horticulture activity as an imposition on them. All the Yanadi requested the anthropologists to give them seeds of bottle gourd and pumpkin though they collected other vegetable seeds too. The Yanadi said that seeds that produce large size fruits were most likeable. They also liked seeds of chillies but this they could get from dried chillies which they purchased every week. The anthropologists felt that if one or two persons in those habitations where the Yanadi were not pursuing horticulture started growing vegetables, others might follow suit as a result of the 'demonstration effect'. They wanted to experiment on this and also wanted to test the viability of cooperative venture among the Yanadi at B.N. Road habitation. A large size plot was taken for this purpose.

Five Yanadi households agreed to work collectively on a plot of 300 square metres. In the initial stage, one person from each household used to work collectively on any particular day but especially on Sundays. They cleared the jungle, hoed the ground and fenced the plot. But they did not sow any seeds as all could not work together. On several occasions one person wanted to go for fishing and the other wanted to go for some purchase. Since one or two persons were missing from the workspot, the remaining ones also refused to work. When asked, they complained against each other and showed no interest in collective work. The Yanadi also expressed their desire to grow vegetables individually. Therefore the anthropologists changed their strategy and started encouraging individual households to grow vegetables. In October 1977, many Yanadi households at Kalavagu, Penubakam, and Pitcharigunta habitations had prepared plots for sowing seeds. During this period, discussion for selection of sites for permanent habitation were in full swing. Though the news that they were going to be shifted soon discouraged many, a few households at Pitcharigunta and Penubakam sowed seeds. But they could not reap the fruits of their labour as they had to move to permanent habitations. However, these Yanadi households began to grow vegetables in their new habitations. Some of the Yanadi prepared small plots on the cultivated land prior to evacuation.

The Public Health Officer, who visits the habitations every week, observed that most of the Yanadi suffered from chronic anaemia and vitamin A deficiency. He advised that the Yanadi should eat drumstick and its leaves and papaya which they could grow easily. Therefore, the anthropologists and two members of the Yanadi Welfare Committee in October 1978 brought nearly 200 branches of the drumstick tree stems available in plenty in the evacuated villages. The Yanadi were informed that whosoever was interested in planting them could take one or two stems. Most of the Yanadi households planted one or two near their huts. But unfortunately most of the drumstick stems could not survive. Later in the fall of 1979, the seeds of the drumstick were distributed and these sprouted well. Forestry and Horticulture Section was also requested to procure some papaya seeds. But before this could be done, a few Yanadi collected some leftover seeds from SHAR employees' housing colonies and sowed them near their huts. In addition, they also distributed papayaseedlings to their relatives.

The Yanadi grow vegetables between October and March. The vegetable plots would be developed near and around a water source. During the monsoon, the ponds and ditches get filled. These are the major sources of irrigation. First, they fence the plot to avoid grazing by stray cattle and goats.

Then the land is dug with a spade and given a spread of goat dung and leaf manure. In a very small area at a corner of the plot, they prepare a nursery bed for raising seedlings of chillies. After a month, the seedlings of chillies are transplanted. Seeds of ridged gourds and brinjal and the like are sown directly near the fence. Some Yanadi plant seeds of bottle gourd near their huts where they usually wash their dishes and take a bath. The plants are watered either in the morning or in the evening. By the first week of March, they harvest chillies which are dried and stored. A few households grow *ragi* millet after harvesting chillies if water is available. In order to encourage vegetable growing, the Yanadi Welfare Committee wished to give prizes to six individuals who showed best performance during 1978-79. The anthropologists suggested to give prizes in kind instead of cash. This suggestion was accepted and three Yanadi were given hens and three were given *dhotis*.

TABLE 7.5 : NUMBER OF HOUSEHOLDS PURSUING HORTICULTURE

Habitation	Number of Households			
	1976-77	1977-78	1978-79	1979-80
Kalavagu	3	6	—	—
Pitcharigunta	2	6	—	—
Penubakam	—	5	30	15
Kothachenu	—	—	20	17
Total	5	17	50	32

Table 7.5 shows a steady rise in the number of households pursuing horticulture. There was a loss of 18 households between 1978-79 and 1979-80. These households temporarily left the habitation to work for the contractors and stayed away during the season of vegetable growing. The Yanadi of Kalavagu and Pitcharigunta settlements shifted to Penubakam and Kothachenu after permanent rehabilitation in 1978 and hence no data in this respect was available for 1978-79 and 1979-80. During 1977, two households harvested enough of chillies for the entire year. In the month of May 1978, one Yanadi made efforts to sow *ragi*. He also encouraged his son-in-law to do likewise. Both of them harvested sufficient quantity of grain to last for a month.

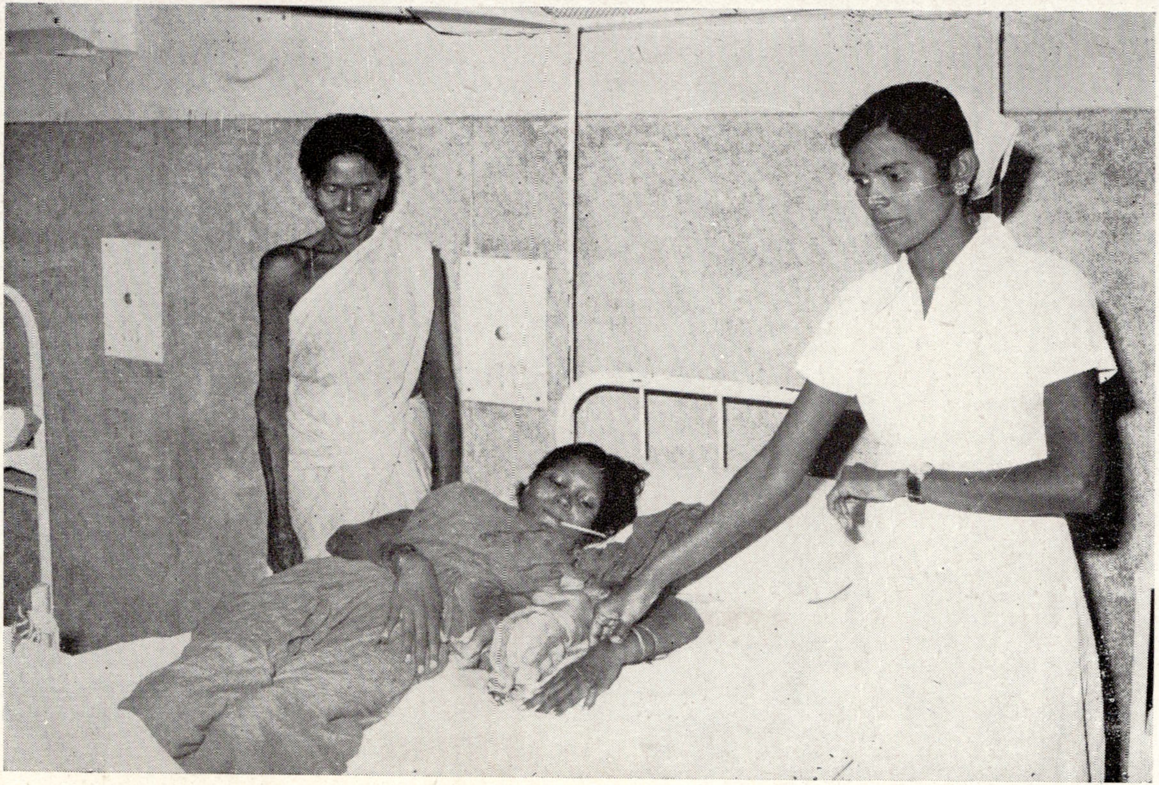

12. A Yanadi mother in hospital

13. The Yanadi Experimental School

TABLE 7.6 : VEGETABLES GROWN BETWEEN 1978-80

Sl. No.	Name of the Vegetable	1978-79			1979-80		
		No. of house-holds	Approximate Quantity (kgs)	Per house-hold	No. of house-holds	Approximate quantity (kgs)	Per house-hold
1.	Chillies	28	92	3.2	16	95	5.5
2.	Bottle Gourd	25	72	2.8	3	37	12.3
3.	Pumpkin	11	72	6.5	—	6	6.0
4.	Ridged Gourd	10	204	20.4	—	—	—
5.	Snake Gourd	5	40	8.0	—	—	—
6.	Sweet Potato	8	25	3.1	1	4	4.0
7.	Brinjal	7	37	5.2	5	39	7.2
8.	Tomatoes	8	32	4.0	3	18	6.0
9.	Watermelon	5	88	17.6	1	—	—
10.	Bendi tubers	4	7	1.7	5	10	2.0
11.	Beans	1	2	2.0	—	—	—
12.	Ragi (Millet)	7	60	8.5	7	118	16.8
13.	Bajra	1	1	1.0	3	8	2.6

During 1978-79, twenty households at Kothachenu and thirty at Penubakam sowed vegetables seeds and chillies. Table 7.6 gives details regarding the amount of vegetables grown by the households. It can be seen that the yield per household increased during 1979-80, even though the number of households was less than that of 1978-79. The reason is that area under horticulture increased during this period.

Domestication of cows

The non-Yanadi of the island possessed cows in large numbers. The cows had been mainly grazing in the forest. They used to let them loose after the milking in the morning while retaining the calves at the home. The cows would come home in the evening.

At the time of evacuation, most of the non-Yanadi could not take their cattle out of the island. The leftovers later moved freely in the forest and multiplied. The anthropologists thought that these cows should be domesticated by the Yanadi. The anthropologists tried to encourage the Yanadi to catch these stray cows and domesticate them. But the Yanadi did not know how to do it. In April 1977, a Yanadi of B.N. Road succeeded in catching a cow and its calf with the help of a non-Yanadi friend. The cow was tied to a tree but it stopped feeding its calf too. The Yanadi was afraid to touch the cow, and therefore, did not attempt to milk it. The calf and cow died after a few days. The anthropologists thought that it might be easy to domesticate a calf instead of a cow. Therefore, the Yanadi were advised to catch a calf. In October 1977, a calf was caught with great difficulty at B.N. Road. The Yanadi tried to domesticate it by feeding grass. But owing to lack of shelter and care, the calf also died, though it was in the process of becoming mild after a month. During November-December 1977, a Yanadi at Penubakam could catch a calf. The mother cow used to feed the calf. The Yanadi tried to catch the mother cow also but could not succeed. During this period, there was continuous rain. Since the calf did not have any shelter, it also died.

A Yanadi at Kalavagu, however, domesticated a wild young calf and looked after it with great care. He shifted to Penubakam along with the calf. The calf used to graze around the habitation and returned to the hut in the evening for two days. But on the third day, it did not return. The Yanadi searched for the calf in the forest, around the habitation and was very much disappointed as he could not find it. He was very sad and expressed his desire to buy a she-buffalo.

These unsuccessful attempts show that efforts in the domestication of stray cattle did not succeed. Further, it shows that only a few Yanadi could take care of the cows even if domesticated ones were provided to them.

Duck rearing

The success in supplementing income through poultry and goats encouraged the anthropologists to suggest the raising of ducks which needed no special skill or training. Even an old person could take care of ducks. The ducks would thrive on worms and snails found in the stagnant water, ditches and streams around the habitation. The ducks could be consumed by the Yanadi. If Yanadi raised more ducks, they could sell the eggs in SHAR labour colonies.

In January 1979, the anthropologists brought three ducks

(two females and one male) for Rs. 23 from a village outside the island. They were loaned to an interested Yanadi of Kothachenu habitation. This Yanadi took great care and daily in the morning drove them to a nearby water ditch and left them there for feeding. In the evening, the ducks returned on their own to the hut. The ducks were also fed with rice bran. He was eagerly looking for eggs. Even after a month, they did not start laying eggs. So, he became apprehensive whether the ducks would lay eggs at all. At this juncture, he wished to return the ducks to the anthropologists. But his son came forward to take care of the ducks. While the old Yanadi was still planning to return the ducks, they started laying eggs after another fifteen days. The Yanadi sold the eggs to a provision shop in Keepakam labour colony at Re. 0.40 per egg. Thus, in three months the Yanadi earned Rs. 50 and returned Rs. 23 (the cost of the birds) to the anthropologists and spent the balance on the household.

In September-October 1979, the Yanadi to whom three ducks were given originally wanted to raise some more ducks. But he required a hen to hatch eggs. The anthropologists made an arrangement by which some eggs could be hatched by the hen of his neighbour. Accordingly, five ducks were raised. The Yanadi could not share the ducks as they do in the case of poultry. They sought the help of the anthropologists to decide the sharing of ducks. Hence, anthropologists divided the ducks as three to the owner Yanadi and two to who ever provided the hen which was agreeable to both of them. Later the Yanadi who got 2 ducks sold them to a Yanadi of Penubakam for Rs. 12 as he found it difficult to rear them. One more Yanadi of Kothachenu purchased five eggs at Sullurpetta and succeeded in getting two ducks in September 1979. One Yanadi of Penubakam purchased ten eggs for Rs. 4 from Kothachenu Yanadi and got them hatched whereby he got seven ducks. Another Yanadi of Penubakam purchased five eggs from outside the island, hatched them and got four ducks. One more Yanadi purchased four ducks for Rs. 25 from a village outside the island. In all, twenty-five ducks were reared by six households by the end of 1979. Thus within ten months, the number of households raising ducks increased from one to six.

Surprisingly, by March 1980, all the eight ducks of Kothachenu vanished in mysterious circumstances. In Penubakam the Yanadi possessed seven ducks in early 1980 and lost four ducks by June 1980. In the months of February-March 1980, the Yanadi of Penubakam purchased four ducks and later in October 1980 sold them to a non-Yanadi outside the island. Thus, by the end of 1980, only four ducks were being reared by two Yanadi households. Failure in raising ducks is not due to the disinterest of the Yanadi, but mostly due to the menace of jackals. A person was required to look after the ducks exclusively. But the Yanadi felt that it was 'uneconomical'.

Fruit collection

The island has a large number of palmyrah and rose-apple trees. Rose-apple and palmyrah trees provide food for the Yanadi. During the season, they are available in such large quantities that most of it goes waste in the forest. Therefore, the anthropologists tried to persuade SHAR administration to permit a few Yanadi to collect the fruits and sell them to SHAR employees. It was hoped that in this way few Yanadi would get livelihood for four months every year. But this request was turned down, as the fruits were considered to be property of the government. It was sad that such an interpretation of law prevented appropriate utilization of natural product. The administrators on the other hand let the fruits go waste in the forest.

The analysis so far indicated that first our attempts centered around SHAR administration to provide employment in one form or other to enhance the level of the Yanadi earning. The Yanadi were provided higher and equal wages and in a very marginal way regular employment. Additional sources of income to daily wages, such as poultry, goats raising, horticulture and duck raising were suggested and implemented to generate new means of survival.

8

Some Other Useful Occupations

IN THE process of change the anthropologists assisted the Yanadi in transferring their dependence from the State Forest Department and private contractors to SHAR Centre. But SHAR Centre is also amenable to external forces beyond the control of the Yanadi and the anthropologists. It was, therefore, considered essential to generate other ways of survival which were independent of SHAR Centre but, at the same time, related to SHAR social environment. They include fishing, setting up provision shops, rearing of milch cattle, and creating leadership among the Yanadi.

Fishing

The Yanadi very much like fishing and eating fish. Traditionally, they fished with bare hands, or with the help of *ootha*, *mandam*, and anglers in ditches, streams, Pulicat Lake, and Buckingham Canal as described in Chapter 4. Five Yanadi households of Kothachenu have taken to fishing for their livelihood since September 1978. Earlier, they had been working with the Forestry and Horticulture Section as casual labourers.

The non-Yanadi staying on the mainland had been fishing in the Pulicat Lake with nets and thus their catch was more than that of the Yanadi of Kothachenu. The Yanadi were selling the fish to the non-Yanadi labourers of Kothachenu. Their earnings ranged from nil to Rs. 10 per day. Yanadi of these households requested the anthropologists to provide them with fishing nets either free of cost or on loan, so that they could catch more and sell to SHAR employees and thereby earn more. During a meeting of the Yanadi Welfare

Committee with the Chairman, ISRO, in October 1978, the desire for fishing nets by Yanadi was mentioned by the anthropologists. The Chairman then requested the Controller to arrange for fishing nets for the interested Yanadi.

When this idea was broached the Internal Financial Advisor suggested the standard procedure of approval and purchase. Accordingly, the anthropologists went to Madras in November 1978 to collect quotations. They failed in this as the prices were fluctuating every day. As an alternative, they suggested cash purchase. But to get cash, a proposal had to be submitted to the Controller once again. Though this was done in November 1978, no action was taken until May 1979 when the anthropologists met the Controller and requested him to approve the purchase of fishing nets in cash. The Controller convened a meeting in which he suggested that the cost of nets may be recovered from the individuals and this money may be used to buy some more nets which could be distributed to other interested Yanadi. In this way, the Yanadi who paid back the cost became the owner of the net. The Controller sent a proposal to the Director for a grant of Rs. 1,200 from the Director's welfare funds. This was granted without any delay. In July 1979, nets were purchased in Madras in consultation with the Yanadi and were given for processing at Sullurpeta. It included fixing beeds on either sides of the net, which was completed in six weeks. On August 23, 1979, the Controller distributed the nets to the six Yanadi. Thus, it took ten months to implement the decision. At Penubakam, the anthropologists encouraged the Yanadi to raise some funds collectively. Accordingly, each household contributed three rupees. With this amount a fishing net was purchased for Rs. 170. The net was put under the custody of a Yanadi. It was agreed that whosoever wanted could use the net for fishing on the condition that each participant in the expedition would get one kilogram of fish and the remaining would be sold. The money thus realized would be kept for common use of a similar kind.

The Yanadi generally go for fishing very early in the morning. If the fishing spot is away from the habitation the expedition starts in the night. The Yanadi sleep near the spot and start fishing early in the morning. They know that the fish move towards the bank of the lake or pond and stagnant water in the morning; when the sun rises the water on the bank gets heated quickly and the fish go deep into the water. Since the Yanadi cannot fish in deep water, they fish in the morning when the fish are on the bank. In shallow water, the Yanadi tie the fishing net across the water, and disturb the water violently. The fish swiftly moving from one side to another are caught in the fishing net. The catch is brought home by afternoon. After keeping some fish aside for household consumption, the remaining fish are sold to non-Yanadi for which there is a ready market in SHAR Centre.

A new problem arose while selling the fish to SHAR employees. The weighing technique followed by the Yanadi was not acceptable to the SHAR employees. So they tried to snatch more fish from the Yanadi. On request, the anthropologists provided the Yanadi with one local balance and some weights. The anthropologists had brought these weights from Madras and gave on cost repayment basis in November 1979. They also taught the Yanadi how to use the weights.

Every evening, the Yanadi sold fish either on cash or credit. Many a time, as soon as the Yanadi returned home with the fish, the non-Yanadi women of the habitation would come to the huts of the Yanadi and purchase the fish. When the fish were caught in large quantities, the Yanadi took them to the SHAR employee, shousing colonies. Initially, the Yanadi complained that the employees commented on the price and quality of fish and sometimes tried to take advantage. The anthropologists told the Yanadi not to worry about this as it was not to insult them and would be set-right in due course of time. The price of fish was always one to two rupees less per kilogram as compared to the price of fish in Sullurpeta. From the earnings, the Yanadi purchased provisions for that evening as well as for the next day. In the case of savings, it was kept for other expenditure or were given to the anthropologists towards repayment. Some money was also saved for dark days and other eventualities.

In order to keep a record of income and loan repayments, the anthropologists gave two small notebooks to each Yanadi. One notebook was meant for keeping income and the other for repayment. Since three of the Yanadi could write in Telugu, this arrangement was made. Documentation was done only for about 25 days, that too in the beginning. In the absence of the anthropologists in November 1979, the loan was repaid to Forestry and Horticulture Section. When the anthropologists returned to SHAR, it was found that only three Yanadi tried to return the loan on three occasions.

Results

Table 8.1 shows the earnings of each Yanadi in the first month by selling fish and the amount returned towards the cost of the net.

TABLE 8.1 : INCOME FROM FISHING AND REPAYMENT OF LOAN IN FIRST MONTH

Case	Income (Rs.)	Repayment (Rs.)
I	285	30
II	187	20
III	150	20
IV	135	20
V	100	20
VI	60	—
Average	151.1	18.3

After a week of fishing, the Yanadi started to repay Rs. 5 to Rs. 10 or whatever and whenever they felt like to the anthropologists. Everyday, the anthropologists visited them and enquired about the catch and told them to quickly repay the loan. They also collected the loan instalments from the Yanadi and entered the figures in the books provided to them. The repaid money was handed over by the anthropologists to the Assistant Administrative Officer in SHAR Centre who was assigned to look after the account.

One Yanadi did not go for fishing regularly, and therefore, earned only Rs. 60. He did not repay anything towards the cost of the net in the first month. Table 8.1 shows that the Yanadi can earn double the amount of what they get in the Forestry and Horticulture Section, if they went regularly for fishing. These six Yanadi had returned Rs. 370 by the end of 1979 towards the cost of the nets. Their income was approximately the same as indicated in the Table 8.1.

From the beginning of 1980, the Yanadi could not catch more fish. The main reason was lack of availability of fish. However, they paid Rs. 126 in total during this year. The important reason for meagre repayment was that the Yanadi required somebody to pursue them to repay the loan. In the absence of the anthropologists in January-April 1980, nobody persuaded the Yanadi to repay the loan. Also during May-June 1980 the movements of the Yanadi were restricted owing to rocket launching. The anthropologists tried to make an alternative arrangement. They thought that the Yanadi could fish in the nothern part of the island during this period. But this required a written permission from the SHAR administration. In May 1980, the anthropologists made a formal request to issue written permission which unfortunately could not be issued. Late commencement of monsoon led to lack of sufficient water and hence fish. Except one Yanadi, the rest worked for the contractors during May-September 1980 and hence could not repay the loans.

At Penubakam, the Yanadi could earn Rs. 120 within three months. On an average, they got Rs. 10 per week by fishing only on Sundays. In addition, each Yanadi who accompanied the expedition got a kilogram of fish.

Financial assistance for independent living

Initially the anthropologists were not much interested in taking financial assistance from the State Government for any developmental activity, because of tenacious formalities, responsibilities, and other difficulties. However, later they had to do so in the absence of other alternatives. Hence in February 1978, the Controller wrote to the Collector, Nellore to explore the possibilities of implementation of some suitable developmental programmes for the Yanadi of Sriharikota.

In response the Collector deputed the Executive Officer, Scheduled Caste Service Co-operative (SCSC) Society to study the conditions of the Yanadi in April 1978. The officer also met some members of the Yanadi Welfare Committee. He suggested state-sponsored programmes like milch cattle, poultry, beekeeping, cane work, carpentry, petty shops, piggery and agriculture. He informed them that the state government would give a subsidy of 25 to 40 per cent of the total investment, depending upon the programme, apart from marginal loan carrying 6.50 per cent annual interest. For the implementation of these schemes, the Yanadi Welfare Committee met the Manager, State Bank of India for additional loans. The manager said that the bank would give loan with 4 per cent interest on the advice of the state government.

In July 1978, the anthropologists met the Executive Officer, SCSC SOCIETY, Nellore and again discussed various developmental programmes. Based on the Yanadi needs, the anthropologists felt that agriculture, piggery, cane work, training in carpentry, beekeeping, and poultry were not viable occupations. As discussed in Chapter 7 agriculture was not possible on the island. Piggery could not be taken up as there was no market. Moreover, it was possible that pigs might become wild as had happened earlier before 1970. For training in tailoring and carpentry, the Yanadi were expected to go to Nellore. Instead some Yanadi showed interest to learn these crafts in Sriharikota itself but the state government was not prepared to send any trainer to do so. Since beekeeping was very risky, this programme was also rejected.

The anthropologists thought that poultry programme could be taken up by the Yanadi. They consulted some experienced persons in SHAR Centre as well as in Sullurpeta and visited a poultry farm at Sullurpeta. It was felt that it would be difficult for the Yanadi to pursue this activity without some training.

The anthropologists felt that milch cattle, provision shops, and bullock cart programme were viable for the Yanadi. Accordingly proposals were submitted for clearance to the Controller in November 1978. These proposals were accepted in principle. The bullock cart proposal was not appreciated by some members of the Yanadi Welfare Committee. The anthropologists proposed this scheme on the ground that there was no private transportation facility for the transportation of personal articles, especially firewood, provisions and household materials. One of the Yanadi was ready to take up this programme. But the members of the Yanadi Welfare Committee were skeptical about the success of the programme. Also later, the interested Yanadi changed his mind and so this programme was abandoned. Applications were submitted in December 1978 to the Executive Officer, SCSC SOCIETY for milch cattle (she-buffaloes) for six Yanadi and two provision shops.

The Executive Officer, (SCSC SOCIETY after a couple of months wrote whether the State Bank, SHAR Centre would sanction loan to these applicants. The Bank Manager took several days in deciding to give loans and informed the Executive Officer in August 1979. The Collector, Nellore, sanctioned loan to all applicants and informed the decision through the Block Development Officer, Sullurpeta to the Yanadi Welfare Committee in September, 1979.

In April 1980, the President of the SCSC SOCIETY sent a demand draft for Rs 1,573 to the Branch Manager, State Bank of India, Sriharikota. He indicated that the amount was the state government's contribution towards loan to eight Yanadi and the balance would have to be met by the Bank. According to the sanction, two Yanadi who had applied for small provision shops would get Rs. 104 each and 6 Yanadi would get Rs. 229 each for buying a she-buffalo. The Branch Manager informed the Yanadi Welfare Committee and requested that arrangements should be made to utilize the loan as soon as possible. However, he asked the committee to stand as surety for a part of the loan given by the Bank.

The President, SCSC SOCIETY while informing the sanction of loan, returned all income and caste certificates to the convenor, Yanadi Welfare Committee as these were not issued by the Tahsildar. The convenor, Yanadi Welfare Committee, requested the anthropologists to complete the formalities. The Block Development Office also informed them that surety could be given by any Yanadi. Therefore, the anthropologists obtained the signature or thumb impressions of the Yanadi who were to get the loan and mutual sureties were given by the applicants. The anthropologists went to the Tahsildar, Sullurpeta in late April and early May 1980 for his signature on the income and caste certificates. But the Tahsildar refused to sign saying that he was not concerned with the Yanadi of Sriharikota and he had no record about the Yanadi of Sriharikota in his office. By using personal influence through a member of the Yanadi Welfare Committee the signatur of the Tahsildar were obtained in mid-May 1980. These forms were later submitted to the Block Development Officer who sent them to the president, SCSC SOCIETY, Nellore.

In the meantime, the Yanadi Welfare Committee discussed as to how to give surety to the Bank. The Manager insisted that unless any responsible officer or the committee guarantees he would not sanction the loan. The members felt that the committee could not give guarantee since it was a voluntary body. Therefore, they convinced the manager that as the state government was accepting the mutual guarantee of a Yanadi so the Bank should accept the same method. Finally he agreed to this proposal and the loans were given to individuals for provision shops and to buy buffaloes.

Provision shops

As indicated in Chapter 5, provision shops were thought to replace mobile provision stores. It is in this spirit that shops were suggested to be opened in each habitation. There were four important points in initiating provision shops to be run by the Yanadi: (i) two households would be able to earn livelihood independently, (ii) it would create the spirit of entrepreneurship, hitherto lacking in most of the Yanadi, (iii) it would help the Yanadi as a group to become self-reliant, and (iv) these petty shops would serve the needs of the Yanadi unlike the mobile provision store which visited the habitations only once a week. Above all it would save the Yanadi from exploitation by the shopkeepers.

Since buying of buffaloes would take time, it was felt that first the two Yanadi who wanted to run provision shops should be given loans. The anthropologists helped them in completing the formalities such as filing of applications to the Bank. Finally, the bank gave two loan cheques each worth Rs. 6C0 in August 1980. On August 4, 1980, the Controller handed over the cheques to the Yanadi in a simple ceremony. The ceremony was arranged in each habitation with the view that other Yanadi will be motivated to receive loans for pursuing some other independent occupations, and also to convince the Yanadi that SHAR Centre was really interested in their economic development. Thupakula Krishnaiah, a Yanadi of Kothachenu habitation showed interest in starting a provision shop and was encouraged by the anthropologists to set up a small shop in his hut in June 1978. He had savings of Rs. 100 with him and borrowed Rs. 100 from a non-Yanadi. With this small amount of Rs. 200 he started the shop. In the beginning, he was finding it difficult to bring provisions from Sullurpeta. He also did not have scales and weights.

The anthropologists requested the SHAR administration to provide him with a balance and weights and permission to purchase provisions through SHAR Employees' Cooperative Stores (SECS) to avoid transportation problems. It was envisaged that SECS would provide provisions at cost price and the Yanadi would sell them on the prevailing SECS rates. The anthropologists requested that SECS should give provisions on credit to the Yanadi. After the sales, the Yanadi would repay the credit before buying any fresh provisions. A part of the profit was also be deposited with SECS for 'capital formation' to make the Yanadi independent in due course of time. But the Secretary of SECS did not agree to this arrangement because he would not get any profit from this deal. Ultimately, the arrangement fell through.

The Yanadi started purchasing provisions from a shopkeeper at Sullurpeta who sold on credit. He bought provisions by bus or truck up to the main gate of the island. He found it very difficult to transport this material from the main gate to Kothachenu. Generally, he hired two or three Yanadi to carry provisions on their heads. He added all this expenditure and a margin of profit to the price. Since his prices were higher, it lead to complaints from the Yanadi of Kothachenu. The anthropologists often verified the prices and the quantity of the items sold to the Yanadi and also discussed all related problems with the Yanadi shopkeeper. The anthropologists helped Krishnaiah to get loan from the state government for expanding his business. The efforts were fruitful in August 1980 when Rs. 600 was sanctioned as described earlier.

The anthropologists felt that instead of handing over the entire quantum to Krishnaiah, it may be given to him in two or three instalments. With his consent, a savings account was opened in the bank and Rs. 600 was deposited. Krishnaiah withdrew Rs. 300 in August 1980 and Rs. 200 in December. Krishnaiah is running his shop very smoothly on fulltime basis. He sells items like chillies, tamarind, salt, matchboxes, cigars, beedis, snuff, onion, groundnut oil, jaggery, and the like mostly used by the Yanadi and non-Yanadi labourers. He has expanded his business by about 50 per cent. His earnings are nearly Rs. 30 per week. He has returned Rs. 400 to the bank. He could have further expanded his business by not repaying the bank loan so quickly. But he felt that he should return the bank loan as early as possible. At the moment, he is ploughing his profits back in the business as earnings of his wife and son are enough for household expenditure.

Loan repayment

Every Monday, Krishnaiah brought Rs. 10 to Rs. 40 to one of the anthropologists to be deposited in the bank. Though the anthropologists explained to him the procedure of depositing, he could not do so on his own. Educating Krishnaiah to deposit money in the bank was considered essential because, in the absence of the anthropologists, he need not depend on others. Before Krishnaiah could learn the deposit procedure the anthropologists had to go away for a short period. So the anthropologists requested the teacher of YES, Penubakam, who lives in Kothachenu to deposit the money in the bank on behalf of Krishnaiah. Having some experience in sales, Krishnaiah maintained up-to-date records of purchase and sales.

Thupakula Kotaiah was another Yanadi in Penubakam habitation who was interested in running a provision shop at Penubakam. Kotaiah had studied up to fifth grade and had worked as *gumastha* (clerk) for the contractors. Thus he could do simple calculations for running a provision shop. Initially he also faced all those difficulties which were faced by Krishnaiah. In the beginning, Kotaiah did not have either a balance or weights or tins and boxes to keep provisions. The Yanadi Welfare Committee was requested to provide a balance and some weights which were lying with them unused. The anthropologists pursued this matter and got a balance, some weights and tins from SECS and gave them to Kotaiah. The anthropologists taught Kotaiah how to use the balance, since it was not a conventional one, and sale of different items of provisions.

Kotaiah also received a loan of Rs. 600. He also bought provisions from SECS to begin with. However, after three months, it was observed that Kotaiah was not running the shop well. The reasons were that he had no prior experience and that he had difficulty in selling provisions. When he returned home after a day's hard work, he preferred to rest than to sell provisions. He did not maintain sales accounts regularly because his eyesight was poor. Since it was almost closed during the day, other Yanadi felt that the shop was not being run. They, however, used it as an alternative to the non-Yanadi shop. Kotaiah's weekly earnings were about Rs. 10. Kotaiah either deposited his money through somebody or brought Rs. 10 every Sunday to the anthropologists to be deposited in the bank. In the absence of the anthropologists, the YES teacher, Penubakam, helped him to deposit the money. By December 1980, Kotaiah had returned Rs. 200 to the bank but most of it was through his daily wage earnings.

At present, Kotaiah works in the Forestry and Horticulture Section as a casual labourer. He runs his shop in the mornings for about two hours and in the evening after 6.00 p. m. If Kotaiah ran his shop on full time basis most of the problems would be solved. Further, the anthropologists requested the YES teacher to help Kotaiah for some time in business matters.

These two Yanadi shopkeepers are not able to sell important items such as rice and kerosene. Only once SECS provided these items to them. It could not supply them regularly because of shortages. The Yanadi of Kothachenu and Penubakam are happy with this facility within their habitation. But they are sore about the lack of rice and kerosene in these shops. At Kothachenu apart from Krishnaiah's shop, there are a few other shops within a range of 1.5 kilometres. In Penubakam, besides Kotaiah's shop there is another shop run by a non-Yanadi who works for a contractor. Because he provides credit facility, some Yanadi buy from his shop. This has affected Kotaiah's sales. The above description demonstrates that occupation of the Yanadi according to their ability and interests could be diversified from forest works. At least one Yanadi household started to lead an independent life. It may be predicted that if we continue similar efforts and provide encouragement, many more Yanadi would take up different occupations.

Rearing of milch cattle

A few Yanadi were interested in rearing buffaloes. They sought the anthropologists' help to acquire buffaloes. They had worked for those non-Yanadi who were rearing buffaloes since childhood. But economic and nomadic life did not permit them to rear a buffalo. They strongly believed that rearing buffaloes would help to increase their income. As discussed earlier when it became certain that loans would be granted the anthropologists started enquiring about the availability of she-buffaloes which could be purchased within the amount of loan sanctioned by the State Bank and the State Government that is Rs. 729. A good buffalo cost more than Rs. 720. They informed the Yanadi Welfare Committee in a meeting of June 1980 that unless the Committee extended some financial assistance, it would not be possible to buy good buffaloes. The committee accepted this suggestion,

Another search for the she-buffaloes was made by anthropologists in August 1980 with the help of two non-Yanadi friends who were very knowledgeable in cattle rearing. They visited three villages near Sullurpeta and finally selected three pregnant she-buffaloes in Sullurpeta itself. The buffaloes were purchased and brought to the island on August 22, 1980. Two of them were purchased for Rs. 810 and Rs. 915 respectively whereas the third one was purchased within the sanctioned loan. Additional funds were made available by the Yanadi Welfare Committee. Each of these buffaloes was selected by the Yanadi individually. The Yanadi did not have any kind of material for rearing the cattle. The anthropologists purchased for each Yanadi a tub, rope, and some bran and hay at Sullurpeta to start the programme. They also requested the non-Yanadi who were familiar with rearing of buffaloes to guide the Yanadi. Out of three buffalo owners, one Yanadi was at Penubakam and the other two at Kothachenu. All three were working in the Forestry and Horticulture Section. After getting the buffaloes, the Yanadi at Kothachenu stopped working. This was because their wives were pregnant and they had to bring grass for the buffaloes. But the Penubakam Yanadi continued to work.

Most of the time, the Yanadi talked about the buffaloes. They carefully observed their feet, body, look and the way of eating. Other Yanadi were carefully watching from their huts as to how the Yanadi were taking care of them. But they would not come close to buffaloes. They were their proud possessions. In the history of the Yanadi, buffaloes were reared for the first time. In the beginning, many non-Yanadi visited the huts of the Yanadi to have a look at the buffaloes. The Yanadi were excited at the comments of the non-Yanadi. Every one eagerly awaited for the delivery of the buffaloes. The first buffalo delivered after three days of its arrival. The Yanadi rushed to the non-Yanadi house with glad tidings and enquired what he was supposed to do now. The non-Yanadi came along with him and explained to him what he should do. The Yanadi performed every activity religiously. The other two owners whose buffaloes had not yet delivered carefully observed and helped.

All the three buffaloes were initially at Kothachenu. A week later, on August 30, 1980, the buffaloes went for grazing and one of them was found missing at noon. The non-Yanadi thought that it might be hiding in the bushes to deliver. The Yanadi searched the bushes but the animal was not found. There was a rumour that buffaloes were stolen regularly from the island and an employee of the post office had lost five buffaloes recently. The Yanadi were frightened very much, so were the anthropologists. The next evening, a non-Yanadi informed them that the buffalo was being held by a non-Yanadi at Kudiri village, six kilometres from the island. The owner Govindaiah, his son-in-law, and the anthropologists went to Kudiri and found the buffalo. The Kudiri villager asked for Rs. 10 for keeping the buffalo safe. The night before, the buffalo had delivered. After paying Rs. 10, Govindaiah brought back the buffalo and the calf to the island. After the buffaloes had delivered, the anthropologists talked to some of the employees who wanted milk. The employees were selected on two criteria. The houses of employees should be close to the huts of the Yanadi and they should be personally known to the anthropologists. Secondly, they should pay the money regularly. The price was fixed as that charged by the non-Yanadi milk vendors i.e. Rs. 2 per litre. The anthropologists felt that it was better if the customers deposited the money in the bank directly as the Yanadi did not know how to deposit the money in the bank. However, the Yanadi required some cash to purchase bran, so a few of the customers were requested to pay in cash.

For measuring milk, the anthropologists procured empty half litre bottles which were given with the instruction that these bottles were of half litre and that this quantity of milk would fetch Re. 1. They were instructed to wash the bottles with warm water and keep them open when empty. The anthropologists told the Yanadi that the women should bring grass and learn milking. The Yanadi women were avoiding these new roles out of fear. The Yanadi were also instructed to gather dung at a place so that it could be sold. After two months, two calves were attacked by bugs. With a Yanadi's help, oil was applied after washing the calves with soap. The calves were later attacked by round worms. One calf survived by the treatment with country medicine. Milking was done twice a day. The Yanadi did not have suitable vessels for milking and they asked the anthropologists to buy some for them. But they were asked to buy it themselves. Each buffalo of Kothachenu Yanadi yielded a little over one litre for two months every morning. One litre was sold and the remaining used. Later, the yield dropped to one litre and the entire quantity was sold. In the evenings, the buffaloes gave only 0.75 litre milk which was also sold. The Yanadi did not supply milk regularly because they were not punctual and also due to lack of appropriate instructions from the customers. They earned Rs. 220 and Rs. 228 by the end of November 1980 and repaid Rs. 70 and Rs. 90 respectively. Each of them had spent Rs. 45 towards bran and *bajra* and the remaining amount was spent on food.

The Penubakam Yanadi was getting 2 litres of milk for the first two months, which was sold regularly. But after two months, the buffalo gave 1.75 litres only. So one and half litres milk was sold and the rest was consumed. He made curd, buttermilk and also learned to make butter. Since then, he did not purchase groundnut oil and had been using ghee instead. His ten-year old son brought the milk from Penubakam to

Keepakam. He walked one way and returned by SHAR bus at 9.15 a.m. But at times, the Yanadi boy was not allowed to travel in the bus. But walking 8 kilometres to and fro was difficult for the boy. So, for the sale of milk in the evening the Yanadi made arrangement with a non-Yanadi to buy it at Penubakam. For two month the buffalo gave one litre, later on it gave only 0.75 litre. By November 1980, the Yanadi had earned Rs. 367 from which he returned the loan of Rs. 245 to the Bank; Rs. 55 was spent towards bran and *bajra*; and the remaining was spent in the house.

The foregoing analysis vividly illustrates the difficulties in introducing the milch cattle programme among the Yanadi. It also indicates that given proper training, encouragement and infrastructural support, the Yanadi can adopt new occupations for independent living. Further, the operational details of the programme are most crucial for successful implementation. At the moment, operational details are left to individuals. It seems that this is one of the serious bottlenecks.

Problems of leadership

The uprooting of Yanadi from the island created a void in leadership and maintenance of harmonious living. The headmen (*maestrilu*) lost their status and controlling power as discussed in Chapter 2. They were no more symbols of power and were not recognized by the new masters of the island since the SHAR administration treated all Yanadi equally. Disputes among the Yanadi were resolved by heads of the households without reinforcement or censure. Some of the decisions were not necessarily considered valid. There were difficulties in controlling these Yanadi whose behaviour was undesirable. Those Yanadi who were dissatisfied with the decisions quietly joined another camp. This situation forced the Yanadi to develop "covert" behaviour to more submissiveness to malign visible beings. It was slowly internalized in their world view as shown in Chapter 3.

When the anthropologists tried to use leaders as entry point there were none to begin with. After the anthropologists gained the confidence of the Yanadi, they were forced into the situation to act as Yanadi leaders. Yanadi's dependence on anthropologists increased for settling disputes, to interact with officials and at times anthropologists were asked to make decisions for Yanadi. In these circumstances the anthropologists very strongly felt that these roles must be assumed by some Yanadi who would continue to live there when the anthropologists left. Sedentary living demanded collective efforts for many community activities leadership to control, regulate, and create collective sense of pride and identity which was lacking among Yanadi. For this purpose also, development of leadership was essential. Keeping these views in mind, the anthropologists started efforts to develop leadership among Yanadi.

To initiate this effort, the anthropologists started inviting older Yanadi whenever a dispute was to be settled in which anthropologist was supposed to make judgement, until September 1977. Afterwards, the anthropologists requested older Yanadi who represented various *intiperu* to pronounce judgement on various disputes. The idea was to develop a *kutam* or village council. But it was observed that older Yanadi started complaining against each other and again the anthropologists were asked to make decisions. However, efforts continued in this direction without much success as same sequence was repeated each time. Efforts were also made to develop another *kutam* in which Yanadi were asked to nominate their *intiperu* leaders as members. Even with this approach, no moral authority of the leaders could be established as they continued to emphasize individual over group. In short, the anthropologists have not been successful in generating any leadership for collective activities. However, efforts will continue as it is considered essential for the future development of the Yanadi.

9

Protection from Illness

As indicated in chapter 4, the Yanadi were not very healthy owing to malnutrition and illness. There were also other reasons for their illness. The Yanadi had little knowledge of modern medicine. They relied on herbal medicine and *rangam* as described in Chapter 3. Little evidence is available to indicate that the Yanadi were exposed to modern medicine prior to 1970 even though it was available on the island at Beripeta. There is a lone case of a Yanadi woman who was seriously injured and was brought to the hospital for treatment. There is no evidence to show that the Yanadi went out of the island for medical treatment. Possibly, it was because their own medical system was able to cater their needs. Also they, being isolated, could not adopt other medical systems available outside the island.

In 1970, when the Yanadi were forced to live on the mainland, their reliance on *rangam* for treatment increased. They were also forced to go to the local doctors and the hospital inducing some of the Yanadi to accept modern medicine. When they returned to the island between 1971 and 1975, some of them had been exposed to modern medicine. A few Yanadi were treated by private doctors at Sullurpeta, whom they found friendly. After their return to the island and before the action project was initiated, the paramedical staff of SHAR Centre made frequent visits to Yanadi camps. This measure was taken to protect SHAR employees from contracting infectious diseases from the Yanadi. The paramedical staff also tried to inoculate Yanadi children as most of them were quite afraid of small pox inoculation. In addition, quinine tablets were also distributed to check the spread of malaria. This was the only medical help extended by SHAR administration to the Yanadi.

The anthropologists convinced the Director, the Controller of SHAR Centre, and the Chairman, ISRO, that the Yanadi should be given medical aid to improve the living standards of the Yanadi. Both preventive and curative medical assistance to the Yanadi was considered essential for the well-being of SHAR employees. On the preventive side, the anthropologists recommended that the doctors and paramedical staff visit Yanadi camps regularly and persuade them to accept modern preventive medicine. On the curative side, it was recommended that the Yanadi should be given free hospitalization along with free food which was generally not given to SHAR employees. Both recommendations were accepted and implemented by the end of 1976. Free hospitalization was, however, provided much earlier than regular visits by the doctors, who believed that patients should come to the doctor.

Free hospitalization

In the beginning no Yanadi came to SHAR hospital for treatment. Only very serious cases were hospitalized, that too, owing to the initiative taken by the Forestry and Horticulture Section officials. Since compulsion would not bring any Yanadi to hospital, it was thought that explaining the advantages of modern medicine would work better.

As discussed in Chapter 3 the Yanadi believed that certain illnesses are caused due to intake of certain foods and water. The anthropologists tried to explain illness and disease in terms of this belief and advised the Yanadi to go to hospital. Without questioning Yanadi about the causes of disease, the anthropologists emphasized that diseases might have been due to biological imbalances or because of intake of wrong food. The Yanadi should also try modern medicine which was nothing but processed herbs and plants. Also medicine could be used along with invocation to gods. It was hoped that effective modern medicine would gradually wean the Yanadi away from their indigenous methods of treatment.

The anthropologists tried to explain about the loss of wages as a result of sickness, and the unending cycle of sickness-no work-loss of wages-insufficient money for food-sickness. The Yanadi were advised to go to the hospital as it would help them to restart their work soon. Some Yanadi expressed that they did not go to the hospital as they did not know how to go through the formalities. Hence, a few Yanadi patients were taken to the hospital by the anthropologists and were told what they should do. Obtaining an out-patient slip and having to state one's age bewildered them. Waiting in a queue also irritated them. They abhorred the idea of collecting urine and faeces for pathological examination. They also found this requirement puzzling.

When a Yanadi entered the hospital, he encountered well-dressed, educated medical personnel. He felt inferior in his 'nudity'. When he went to the doctor, he stood some distance away from him and hesitated to sit on the chair. The Yanadi felt the doctors' behaviour impersonal and found it difficult to answer such questions as 'the number of days' or 'time'. There was also a problem of language as there are dialectical variations in Telugu and some doctors were actually non-Telugu speakers. The Yanadi could not verbalize all their complaints and the doctors found it difficult to comprehend them. A few Yanadi came to the hospital for follow-up. Some of them preferred to go to private clinics at Sullurpeta where there were no formalities and where some sort of friendliness existed due to prior contacts. To overcome these difficulties, the anthropologists accompanied the Yanadi to hospital on several occasions.

In an emergency, the anthropologists called for the ambulance. Some patients left the hospital half way through the treatment. Observations indicated that the Yanadi did not like to be admitted to the hospital. For them, hospital environment was alien and involved interaction with strangers who were superiors. They felt lost in such a situation. The Yanadi also felt lonely in the hospital and children did not like to be kept away from their parents. If a Yanadi was admitted, another person was required to stay with the patient for assistance, which meant loss of wages for that person also.

The hospitalized Yanadi were given free meals from the SHAR canteen. This facility was discontinued from March 1978.

The anthropologists brought this to the notice of the Controller and requested him to continue to provide free meals to the Yanadi patients. SHAR administration re-introduced free meals to the hospitalized Yanadi from October 1978. During the interregnum, expenditure on meals for Yanadi patients, was met by the Yanadi Welfare Fund. From April 1979, onwards some restrictions were imposed on the medical aid. The Yanadi out-patients were given certain medicines free of charge. But the cost of some other medicines was recovered. This made the Yanadi unhappy. However, hospitalized Yanadi were given all medicine free of cost. The efforts of the anthropologists yielded good results as the Yanadi slowly began to avail of treatment at SHAR hospital (see Table 9.1). Of the 26 patients admitted in 1977, three died in the hospital and one out of eight in 1980. Deaths in the hospital were not attributed to the negligence of the doctors or to the bad treatment. In the Yanadis' opinion only helpless patients were brought to the hospital. Table 9.1 shows that in the subsequent years

TABLE 9.1 : COMPLAINTS OF PATIENTS HOSPITALIZED DURING 1977-80

Complaint	1977			1978			1979			1980		
	M	F	T	M	F	T	M	F	T	M	F	T
Fever/*Janni* *	13	6	19	6	4	10	2	3	5	—	1	1
Delivery	—	4	4	—	5	5	—	2	2	—	5	5
Snakebite/Attack of wild bull	1	—	1	—	—	—	—	1	1	—	—	—
Hydrocele Operation/Fits	1	—	1	—	1	1	—	—	—	—	—	—
Tuberculosis	—	—	—	1	—	1	1	—	1	—	1	1
Toothache/Chest pain/pains	—	1	1	2	—	2	2	—	2	1	—	1
Total	15	11	26	9	10	19	5	6	11	1	7	8

M=Male; F=Female; T=Total

* Local name of a disease which leads to low temperature of the body.

there was a gradual decrease in the number of patients admitted to the hospital. The reason for this was that the Yanadi did not fall seriously ill as they did before 1978. Perhaps this may be attributed to medicines being supplied at their doorstep when they fell sick. Thus, it can be said that the health of the Yanadi has improved in last four years.

Taking medicare to the Yanadi doorstep

Because of the poor response of the Yanadi to modern medicine and hospitalization in the beginning, it became imperative for anthropologists to evolve a new strategy to protect the Yanadi from illness. Anthropologists discussed the problem of the Yanadi at SHAR hospital with the Controller in February 1977, and requested him to arrange transportation facilities to the Yanadi from their camps to hospital. During the discussion it was decided by the Controller that SHAR hospital doctors would visit approachable Yanadi camps and provide treatment to them twice a week. The anthropologists welcomed this new strategy. The doctors went to the Yanadi instead of the Yanadi coming to the doctor. This was thought to be the best method to protect the Yanadi from illness, at least in the beginning. The doctors did not welcome this idea initially. This practice started in March 1977.

The team of the medicare staff consisted of a Public Health Officer (trained medical doctor), a nurse, a pharmacist, a public health supervisor, and a public health assistant along with either an *ayah* or an attendant. All of them were trained paramedical staff. This makeshift mobile clinic was equipped with chairs, a wash basin, medical chest and other medical equipments. From March 1977 till the permanent settlement, the mobile clinic visited the Yanadi camps on Mondays and Thursdays in the morning. Two camps were visited each day.

The mobile clinic did not function from December 1977 to February 1978 due to non-availability of the doctors. It was re-started from the third week of February 1978. The new doctor who accompanied the clinic suggested that in order to serve the Yanadi more effectively the clinic should be run in the evenings when all the working Yanadi returned home after the day's work. For some time the clinic was run in the evenings, but these evening visits were withdrawn due to certain administrative difficulties. It stopped functioning altogether in April 1978, due to shortage of doctors. It resumed working in the third week of July 1978 and functioned regularly until May 1980. The mobile clinic did not function for the next six months due to lack of doctors. After the permanent settlement of the Yanadi camps, the mobile clinic discontinued visits to Kothachenu but continued to visit Penubakam habitation on Fridays in the afternoons.

Generally, the vehicle was parked in the habitation where patients came out in the open for treatment. The announcement of its arrival was done by a long hoot of the horn helped by the children who shouted about the arrival of 'hospital'. The Public Health Officer asked the children to announce their arrival and call out the patients. After setting up the clinic the Public Health personnel would call for patients. The very visit of the clinic created a certain amount of commotion in the Yanadi habitation. Young children would be scared, the relaxing Yanadi would be alerted and they would hurry to meet the doctor. The doctor sat on a chair, and asked the Yanadi to do so which many of the Yanadi refused to do as a mark of respect. After the examination, medicine was prescribed which was supplied by the pharmacist. Injections were avoided as the doctors thought that the Yanadi would be afraid of them. Again it was economical and more practical to give oral medication to the Yanadi.

It was observed quite often that the Yanadi would approach the doctor just before he started packing up or just before his departure. This annoyed the doctor but the Yanadi got themselves examined and obtained the medicine, unaffected by the doctor's annoyance. It was observed that the doctor seldom touched the patients or conducted any physical examination. If the doctor was a non-Telugu speaker, he manage to communicate through sign language or through one of the paramedical staff. In the case of a serious patient, the doctor asked the patient to report to the hospital on the following day. Most of the Yanadi did not follow the instructions of the doctors but things have changed recently.

After the examination, the doctor and the paramedical staff made a quick inspection of the habitation if time permitted. On these inspections, the doctor who worked between

1978 and 1980 asked about the welfare of those patients who were treated earlier or those who were suffering for a long time. He also checked the hygiene at the habitation and made some suggestions. These visits were extremely useful in developing personal relationships and in generating a sense of confidence among the Yanadi about the doctor. After completion of the visit, the mobile clinic returned to the hospital. These visits have become part of the Yanadi life style.

The anthropologists continuously acted as a link between the hospital and the Yanadi and assisted both in several ways. In mid-1978 when the anthropologists suspected that five of the Yanadi had leprosy, they informed the Public Health Officer. So the doctor conducted a survey and by early 1979 they could detect 16 Yanadi suffering from leprosy and five 'contact's. The 'contact' is a person who stays with the leprosy patient in the same hut, and such a person is also treated as a preventive step. Out of 16, one Yanadi died in early 1980. Of the 15, eight patients are being given treatment regularly till now and the treatment for the rest of the seven was discontinued because of their continuous non-availability in the habitation. Out of the five contacts, two have stopped and three have continued the treatment. The paramedical staff delivers the medicine on the scheduled days at the patients' huts.

In August 1978, the Public Health Officer arranged a film show on leprosy in Kothachenu and Penubakam habitations. The film show made a strong impact on the patients. Earlier these patients were not keen in taking medicines even when these were supplied at their huts. But after the film, they started going to hospital for medicine after the dose was over. The results of the medication for leprosy were very significant. The Yanadi were very happy about recovering from this disease which they thought was incurable. The Public Health Officer assured the anthropologists that leprosy among the Yanadi would be completely controlled very shortly.

In November 1978, the Public Health Officer arranged BCG vaccination for the first time in the history of the Yanadi. The response of the Yanadi was also encouraging. All school children and adults below 20 years of age were inoculated. Most of the Yanadi came forward to get themselves inoculated unlike the anti-cholera inoculation in November 1977.

The SHAR hospital launched a family planning campaign in October 1979. The medical staff tried to motivate the Yanadi women to adopt family planning methods and persuaded some for loop insertion with due help from the anthropologists. The anthropologists also tried to explain to the Yanadi the importance of a small family and its usefulness. Though at present the Yanadi households are small (3.8 persons per household), the family planning programme introduced the concept of spacing between children.

Insertion of loop was considered an operation by the Yanadi women. In order to remove their doubts, the medical staff demonstrated the process of loop insertion on a non-Yanadi woman. In spite of the demonstration, the Yanadi women showed unwillingness to adopt it. The medical staff also screened a few films on family planning. But the Yanadi could not comprehend the messages of these films.

Drinking water

Before evacuation, the Yanadi drank water from ditches and wells. These wells were constructed by the State Government. When there was no well close by, the Yanadi dug ditches two or three metres deep which they called *chelimelu* or *guntalu* and fixed a hollow stump of a palmyrah tree. Water from the ditches was collected into pitchers. During summer when the water table would go down, then the Yanadi would have to dig deeper.

The anthropologists felt the need for having handpumps to provide filtered and clean water. They requested SHAR administration to provide handpumps in various Yanadi camps. This suggestion was accepted and by December 1976 nine handpumps at Pitcharigunta and one at B.N Road camps were installed. Out of eight Yanadi camps only two camps were provided with handpumps. The Yanadi in the remaining camps continued drinking water from ditches. Handpumps were seen by the Yanadi for the first time when they were installed by SHAR administration in 1970. From then, the Yanadi saw the operation of handpumps by the non-Yanadi. When the Yanadi were employed in the Forestry and Horticulture Section they had to use handpumps to draw water at some places. That is how they got acquainted with handpumps. So when handpumps were installed in 1976, the Yanadi rather welcomed the idea.

When Solladaruvu Yanadi were shifted to B.N. Road settlement, the increased in the population necessitated the installation of another handpump which was installed at B.N. Road camp in February 1977. In a short report submitted to the Controller in April 1977, water problem in other camps was highlighted. So in May 1977, a handpump was installed at Kalavagu camp. The Yanadi of Penubakam requested anthropologists many a time to provide them with a handpump. But this was not possible as Penubakam was located in the interior of the forest.

While planning for new permanent settlements, the anthropologists suggested that each settlement should be provided with two wells apart from several handpumps. Wells were to act as stand by to handpumps. After resettlement Penubakam and Kothachenu were provided with five and seven handpumps respectively and two wells each. For drawing water from wells, often a small tin bucket and rope were provided by SHAR administration. A plumber and a helper from Civil Maintenance Section visits each habitation once a week to attend to repairs. In the beginning, the anthropologists informed the concerned officials when a handpump went out of order. But now the Yanadi themselves take initiative to get them repaired. In some cases, they also attend to minor repairs with the little knowledge they have gained by now. The Yanadi now have completely stopped drinking ditch water. Water from wells is mostly used for bathing and washing clothes at Kothachenu as it is unfit for drinking. At Penubakam even though well water is fit for drinking, the Yanadi mostly drink water from handpumps. It is observed that wells are being used mostly by those Yanadi who stay near to them.

During April-May 1980, there was difficulty in drawing water from handpumps as the water table had gone down. Failure of the monsoon aggravated the situation. In May-June all handpumps in Kothachenu and Penubakam habitations were deepened. An additional handpump was provided at Kothachenu on the request of the anthropologists.

The important factors as to why the Yanadi completely discontinued the use of ditch water and started using the water from handpumps in the habitations are (i) it is very easy to draw water from the handpumps, (ii) the maintenance of the handpumps is looked after by the Civil Maintenance Section of SHAR Centre; and (iii) the water from the handpumps is considered cleaner than the ditch water.

Special nutrition programme

CARE (Co-operative for American Remittances to Everywhere) is running a special nutrition programme for the tribals of Andhra Pradesh. Under this programme, children below six years of age, nursing mothers, and pregnant women are provided with 200 grams of *upma* (made of semolina) every morning excepting Sundays. This programme was extended to the Yanadi by the Block Development Officer, Sullurpeta as it was expected to help improve health standards of the Yanadi.

The programme is administered in Kothachenu habitation by the school teacher. He receives Rs. 20 per month as remuneration. A Yanadi woman is employed of Rs. 40 per month to cook and distribute food and clean utensils. The Special Nutrition Programme started in April 1978. It is continuing with intermittent breaks. The number of beneficiaries of the programme has gone up to fifty.

In the beginning, there were complaints raised by the Yanadi about this programme. One of them was that it was not sufficient to last the whole day. *Upma* was an early morning meal and the Yanadi women thought that it should be sufficient for three or four servings. Another misconception was that since earlier at Thakkar Bapa Gurukulam at Jonangipalem, Yanadi children were served three meals a day, the women felt that their children too should be fed three times a day. The anthropologists explained that *upma* given was more to improve their health than as a substitute for their meals. Initially, some children suffered from diarrhoea as they were not accustomed to such a diet.

Today, by any standard, regular medical assistance both preventive and curative, has helped to protect the Yanadi from illness. At the same time, it has improved the survival ability of the Yanadi in the changed circumstances. There is a fairly good chance that a Yanadi would not die on the island owing to lack of medical assistance. Adoption of modern medicine among the Yanadi is the result of a number of forces acting simultaneously. These include their evacuation from the island, non-availability of herbs on the mainland, and initial positive experience by a few from private doctors on the mainland. The strategy to brings doctors to the doorsteps of the Yanadi and the doctors' sympathetic attitudes towards Yanadi became an important factor for the acceptance of modern medicine. Above all the persuasion of anthropologists for adopting modern medicine while respecting 'indigenous' methods of treating helpedthem to accept the change. Analysis of world view and its implication in understanding the concept of illness helped anthropologists in persuadingh the Yanadi to accept modern medicine. It would not be out of place to mention that the Yanadi were ready to accept any change if it would improve their chances of staying on the island.

10

Learning for Futurc

AN ATTEMPT has been made in this monograph to describe the methods and means followed in last five years for assisting the Yanadi in their quest for survival in the changed environment and among alien people. Our dual role that served as a master spirit was that of researcher and change agent. In the second role, we acted as partners and collaborators in bringing about the resultant effects of each effort set out in Chapters 5-9 without integrating into a whole to understand the total impact either qualitatively or quantitatively. In the concluding Chapter, we will like to view the entire action programme as an integrated whole. We would also like to bring out some of the salient experiences which might be helpful to researchers like us making similar attempts in action anthropology.

Yanadi today

The Yanadi today is confident and feels secure on the island. They are far removed from the perpetual state of anxiety and helplessness. They meet security personnel and non-Yanadi with ease and with a sense of dignity and equality. The Yanadi today retaliate if anybody tries to harass them. The non-Yanadi complain that the Yanadi are no more submissive and subservient as they used to be. By and large, they live in the two habitations, which are more or less similar to their earlier habitations except that they have shrunk and are crowded.

The Yanadi today are able to have at least two square meals a day from their earnings. The number of starvation days in the Yanadi life have decreased so much so that a Yanadi does not go to sleep without food of some kind or other. There are ample evidences that the modest efforts put in have permitted a steady and continuous income from sources other than forest leading to a lesser amount of uncertainty and dependence on exploitative forces beyond the Yanadi control. Due to sedentary living, new occupations, schooling of children and increased cereal intake the Yanadi dependence on the forest have reduced in spite of the fact that they live in the midst of forest. Forest collection of fire wood, fruits and roots, however, continue to be an important pastime activity for the Yanadi.

In general, the Yanadi are exposed to various new ideas as a result of continuous interaction with the non-Yanadi and their ways of living. This includes exposure to mass media also. The acquaintance and mere seeing of the ISRO activities through rockets, electronic gadgets, and other equipments directly or indirectly have started influencing the Yanadi-world view and life. Observations have indicated that these have lead to change in dream patterns of the Yanadi. They have started dreaming about the sound and thunder of rocket firing.

The dependence on SHAR administration for survival has been brought down as a result of taking to fishing, dairy, and small business. These developments took place due to multi-prone attack on exploitation and the vicious cycle of exploitation. Once the Yanadi came out of this vicious cycle, even their meagre earnings were able to provide them two square meals. Higher and equal wages have added to their better living. But then Yanadi started drinking country liquor which was not commonly known to them prior to the taking over of the island and have been prohibited by the SHAR administration.

As a result of accepting modern preventive and curative medical system provided by SHAR administration, today no Yanadi would die due to lack of medical facilities. On the contrary, in a very short span, Yanadi have learnt to use modern medicines for their survival without abandoning their old belief system. Introduction of modern medicine came about by analysing the Yanadi world view and using its positive concepts for introducing the modern medicines.

With certain amount of 'subjectivity' we like to assert that

Yanadi today are leading a better life than prior to initiating the action project. The quality of life has improved so much so that without losing identity, they are able to accept new ways and means for survival. These new means and ways have brought about changes in physical environment, food habits, clothing but without affecting their individualistic life style and freedom that the Yanadi cherished most. It is expected that the Yanadi would accept further changes. But no matter what changes take place, the Yanadi will make their own decisions before accepting or rejecting them. It is this kind of independent decision-making ability that have helped Yanadi to maintain their identity and independence without being dependent upon SHAR administration.

Some lessons learnt

Almost all programmes that were implemented during last five years, had long gestation period. The longest effort being of nearly twenty months in providing permanent passes to Yanadi. Same is the case in securing loan for buying milch cattle, scholarships for students, distribution of fishing nets, selection of permanent habitation and many other programmes. Further, analysis indicated that the long duration of gestation period is closely associated with the existing procedure and undefined role of various agencies involved in the implementation of the programmes. For an efficient implementation of programmes, it is essential that the gestation period must be reduced which can be done by providing appropriate authority or financial support to the project implementors.

There is ample evidence in Yanadi culture to characterize it as a 'non-competitive' culture. As a result of induced changes, the Yanadi have imbibed some 'sense of competition' among themselves and with other non-Yanadi. There is no doubt that we have been responsible for this, but it was done so that the Yanadi could face the expanding horizons of their new world beyond the island. We have yet to know whether it would lead to new conflicts in the Yanadi life style and values.

The process that was followed to assist Yanadi in the changed circumstances provided us a unique experience and insight that could be utilized in other similar circumstances. It is very important to focus the plight and the state of helplessness of Yanadi when we met first. The Yanadi were rootless and had lost sense of direction. At the same time, they were harassed by others in very many ways. In such a situation, they were ready to accept any idea or change that would help them to stay in the island. In our opinion, the compelling needs to stay in the island was a critical factor in accepting anthropologists as their 'friends'. So the successes of various programme implementations must not solely be attributed to the efforts of the anthropologists.

Further, the traumatic experience of being 'homeless' created serious 'psychological' problems more than 'economic' problem. The identification of such a problem and its removal was probably the stepping stone for all the efforts that were made to assist Yanadi. It is therefore, very important to analyse the needs and problems of the 'traget group' for providing meaningful help even before initiating any programme.

Based on the need assessment analysis, several ideas were suggested by anthropologists. But only few could be implemented in which no more than couple of them really helped the Yanadi in improving their economic condition. The experiences suggest that the anthropologists must make a multi-prone attack to help the community in distress, rather than just follow, a single line of action. While doing so, a clear philosophical stand must be taken for defining the direction of desired change. Such a view assumes that there is a very little scope for 'value free' position for anthropologists in any action situation.

Our experiences show that the introduction of any change in any aspect of a culture is a collective effort of many agencies which in the present case were SHAR Centre, State Government Yanadi Welfare Committee, anthropologists and Yanadi themselves. It seems that the coordination and co-operation is essential for the success of any developmental programme. The anthropologists with the help of others were able to achieve certain goals which would have been difficult to achieve otherwise.

Analysis of culture provided very important clues while imparting education to Yanadi children. Learning through demonstration and imitation was found to be the most effective.

'Experimental approach' further contributed in successful implementation of educational programme. It is suggested that as far as possible 'experimental approach' should be followed especially in the initial stages of the programme implementation. This study may be construed merely as a mid-programme evaluation because our efforts continue as an attempt in action anthropology.

Bibliography

Bastide, Roger : *Applied Anthropology*. Translated by Alice L. Morton. London : Croom Helm, 1973.

Census of India 1961 : *Andhra Pradesh, Series 2 Parts X-A and B. (Village and Town Directory) Nellore District*. Hyderabad : The Government of Andhra Pradesh.

Census of India 1961 : *A Monograph on Rettamala (Sullurpeta Taluka, Nellore District), Vol. II, Andhra Pradesh, Part VI* (Village Survey Monographs, Serial No. 25). Delhi : Controller of Publications.

Census of India 1971 : *Andhra Pradesh, Series 2 Parts X-A and B (Village and Town Directory), Nellore District*. Hyderabad : The Government of Andhra Pradesh.

Clifton, James A (ed.) : *Applied Anthropology*. Boston : Houghton Mifflin Company, 1970.

Foster, George M. : *Applied Anthropology*. Boston : Little, Brown & Company, 1969.

Goodenough, Ward H. : *Cooperation in Change*. New York : Russell Sage Foundation, 1963.

Indian Space Research Organisation : *Weather Over* SHAR*—Part I (Surface Data)* by R. Venkataraman et. al. SHAR : ISRO, 1979.

Mair, Lucy : *Applied Anthropology*. London : London School of Economics, 1968.

Naik, T.B. : "Applied Anthropology in India." In *A Survey of Research in Sociology and Social Anthropology* (Vol. III). Bombay : Popular Prakashan, 1972.

Nellore Manual : *Letters Relating to Shriharikota Yanadis*. Proceedings of the Madras : Madras Presidency, Board of Revenue, 1846-1882.

Peddington, Ralph : "Action Anthropology". In *Applied Anthropology*, (ed.) James A Clifton, Boston : Houghton Mifflin Company, 1970.

Raghavaiah, V. : *The Yanadi.* New Delhi : Bharatiya Adimjati Sevak Sangh, 1964.

Rao, E. Venugopal : *Working Plan for the Forests of Shriharikota Group of Islands (namely Shriharikota, Pernad and Venad Islands), 1967-68 to 1976-77.* Nellore: Government of Andhra Pradesh (Mimeographed), 1970.

Redfield, Robert : *The Primitive World and Its Transformations.* Ithaca : Cornell University Press, 1953.

Redfield, Robert : *The Little Community.* Chicago : University of Chicago Press, 1955.

Tax, Sol : "The Fox Project" in *Applied Anthropology.* (ed.) James A. Clifton. Boston : Houghton Mifflin Company, 1970.

Thurston, E. : *Castes and Tribes of South India* (Volume VII). Madras : Government Press, 1909.

Vidyarthi, L.P. : "Anthropology and Tribal Policy : A Case Study among the Maler, Paharia : Some Preliminary thoughts". In *Indian Anthropology in Action*, ed. L.P. Vidyarthi. Ranchi: Ranchi University, 1960.

Vidhyarthi, L.P. : *Rise of Anthropology in India* (Vol. II). Delhi: Concept Publishing Company, 1978.

Index